Tribal Secrets

Tribal Secrets

Recovering American Indian
Intellectual Traditions

Robert Allen Warrior

 University of Minnesota Press

Minneapolis

Contents

Acknowledgments

Writing this book has required many kinds of support, and I am grateful for all of it. At Union Seminary, where the book had its beginnings as a doctoral dissertation, Geoff Johnson, Sally McNichol, Professor James Washington, Nan Haxby, Ken Spence, Immanuel Marty, Terry Todd, and Professor Delores Williams each played a part in its completion. Steven Ray Smith, who understands the travails of writing, heard about the project every step of the way. A more sympathetic listener or better friend cannot be imagined. Lance Friis and Carla McDonough have also been good friends throughout the project. Lisa Freeman, Todd Orjala, Laura Westlund, Ellen Foos, and the rest of the wonderful and patient staff at the Press have been a joy to work with.

Many American Indian people have inspired me to keep going, even when I was considering changing course. Donna Chavis, Steve Roberson, Carole Butler, Debra Smith, and Ray Cook have provided various forms of support and advice. American Indian students and staff at Stanford University, especially Jim Larimore, Denni Woodward, Beverly Corriere, and Anne Medicine, have made my teaching and work an inspiring and rewarding challenge.

Various Osage people and their families gave me little choice but to remain at my keyboard, often just by checking on the progress of the work. Marian Cass, Browning and Sharon Pipestem, Cora Hickey, Cecelia Tallchief Lemon, and Kathryn, Charlie, Jeri, Yancey, and Moira Red Corn provided valuable support and generous hospitality. Tahlee Red Corn's suspicion of Indian academics, along with his generosity and friendship in the summer of 1991, kept me honest as I wrote. He is also the only person who has ever explained Einstein's theory of relativity to me in terms I could understand. Being able to write much of this manuscript living among such fine people was both an honor and a pleasure.

Members of my extended Osage family have encouraged me in more ways than they know. Archie Mason Jr. and Ramona Mason have given me a sense of the value of both Anglo and traditional Osage education. Arita Jump, Flora Jump Quinata, and Meredith Quinata provided an occasional phone call, an encouraging note, and chicken-fried steak in Wynona.

Special thanks are due to those who read the following work in its various, often extremely rough, drafts. Melissa Aase, John Buggeln, and Gideon Khabela provided important insights. Eduardo Mendieta's adversarial, detailed analysis still raises troubling questions in my mind. A. LaVonne Brown Ruoff provided a tough but fair reading that corrected and strengthened the work, as did Elaine Jahner. Jace Weaver and Paul Chaat Smith have been in many ways my better selves as readers.

In the English department at Stanford University, Suvir Kaul, Ramon Saldivar, Jay Fliegelman, David Halliburton, and Albert Gelpi read drafts or portions of drafts. George Dekker, Horace Porter, Sandra Drake, Ron Rebholz, Lora Romero, Sharon Holland, and Jay Grossman have been especially helpful colleagues. Their insights and suggestions were of tremendous help in the later stages of revision. Students in three seminars that covered aspects of this work provoked my thinking and helped me clarify much of what follows.

One of the most rewarding aspects of this early stage of my academic career has been the experience of having so many senior American Indian scholars come to my aid and encourage me to continue. Terry P. Wilson, Inés Talamentez, William Willard, Gerald Vizenor, Elizabeth Cook-Lynn, and George Tinker read the manuscript in various forms and provided valuable comments. Reaves Nahwooks, Clydia Nahwooksy, Betty Parent, and many others helped me both with content of the manuscript and with existential vocational struggles. Kate Shanley's comments on the manuscript for the University of Minnesota Press were both incisive and encouraging. Vine Deloria Jr. responded graciously to various questions about his work. More than anything else, all of these scholars have served as examples of how to be serious about the work we do while not taking ourselves too seriously.

James Cone, from the moment we first met, has never altered course in his support of my work. Few dissertation advisers would have given me the freedom he did in allowing my research and writing to unfold in the way that they did. His commitment to scholarly excellence, responsible teaching, and engaging love for his own people will continue to serve as a sobering influence on me. He has given me a gift the burden of which I will never stop carrying. To him and all of the wonderful readers, I am grateful. Whatever problems remain, of course, all belong to me.

My mother and father deserve special honor. Though he could not have imagined that I would someday write a dissertation about them, my father, Allen Warrior, was the person who first introduced me, via his bookshelves, to both Deloria and Mathews. The support of my mother, Judy Warrior, has been vital throughout my academic life.

Margaret Kelley (and Indigo the dog) has shared my life and thus this work. She has indulged my obsession with the manuscript and provided a sounding board for various conceptual problems I have confronted along the way. Her love, respect, and patient spirit have helped me through many difficult days.

My brother, David Warrior, died of AIDS-related pneumonia before I could complete this project. I am thankful that he lived long enough to see the dissertation version and its dedication to him. He was my first and best teacher. Whether I needed personal advice, a distracting conversation about musical theater, or an ear to listen to my latest intellectual meanderings, he was always there. From the day his "Robbie Baby" came home from the hospital, he never wavered in his support of my life, my work, and my joy. I miss him terribly. Of all the revisions I have made in this work, the ones on the dedication page were by far the most difficult.

Redwood City, California
New York City
Pawhuska, Oklahoma

Introduction

This work is a comparative interpretation of the works of Vine Deloria Jr. (Standing Rock Sioux) and John Joseph Mathews (Osage),
two American Indian intellectuals of this century. In bringing these
two thinkers together I am interested in laying the groundwork for
a discussion of several crucial issues in contemporary American Indian critical studies. This introduction will make explicit the trajec-
tories of the work and indicate the questions and concerns that have
prompted it.

Tribal Secrets is concerned with several questions. First, to what
extent do the various conceptual and analytical categories currently
available in American Indian scholarship provide an adequate
framework for the emergence of a mature Native cultural and literary criticism? Second, what impact can the increasing awareness of
and engagement with American Indian writers of earlier periods
have upon the way contemporary Native intellectuals develop
Indian critical studies? Concomitantly, how does construing the
field in the terms of intellectual history rather than literary or
generic history change the critical landscape? Finally, how much
responsibility do Native intellectuals of today have for addressing
such issues as economic and social class, gender, and sexual orientation within Indian life, issues that have been for the most part
overshadowed by academic and popular fascination with Native
Americans?

This present work is not a complete answer to any of these questions. Rather, I argue throughout that the ways in which answers to
these questions emerge is as important, finally, as the answers themselves. The development of a framework through which engagement

with issues central to the future of Indian critical studies can occur is thus my primary focus.

That framework issues from my comparison of Deloria and Mathews. Finding such critical language and categories is the major thrust of the writings of both figures, making them ideal subjects for critical scrutiny and constructive engagement. Of the two, Deloria is the better known. His ground-breaking *Custer Died for Your Sins* (1969) and subsequent books and essays from the early 1970s established him as the leading contemporary American Indian intellectual figure. His sometimes biting, always insightful and incisive commentaries on the United States and Indian America have impacted the shape of both federal Indian policy and Indian self-understanding. One quotation that shows him at his best comes from recent comments, in the midst of an essay about religious freedom, on non-Native fascination with American Indian spirituality:

> Indians, of course, come as an afterthought. Their religions are considered exotic, primitive, and precisely the kind of spirituality that many Christians wish they could find in their own rituals. Indeed, annually we are treated to many conferences in which American Indians are asked to speak about spirituality. We see Episcopal bishops garbed in outlandish purple vestments, with war bonnets on their heads, trying to hold a communion service that is partially Christian and partially pow-wow. We see hundreds of Christian clergy coming to the reservations like Nicodemus at night, trying to get into sweat lodges and sun dances so they can have some kind of religious experience. It is all too sad.[1]

Mathews, though not as well known, also produced an impressive body of literature. He was born in 1894 on the Osage Reservation of Oklahoma Indian Territory and earned degrees at the University of Oklahoma and at Oxford University. He died in 1979. His softer-edged literary elegance complements Deloria's sharp tone. He speaks of cooking meals for friends in his masterpiece, *Talking to the Moon*:

> Standing in shorts and cowboy boots at the kerosene stove, I am happy. The sweat pours from my face and body, and I have a towel around my neck and a glass of whiskey and soda or a bottle of beer at hand, which the hungrier guests keep supplied

as an excuse to see how the food is coming. Only people who have never visited the Blackjacks before ever come into the kitchen to offer advice, some visitor who has reached the egg-frying or the spaghetti stage in the beautiful art.[2]

In this and in his other books Mathews shows himself to be a keen literary observer of the complex biological and social life around him.

The impressive oeuvres of Deloria and Mathews have not provoked among students of American Indian literature and history much critical literature about either figure. Less than a dozen sources exist about Mathews and his work, three of those being concerned primarily with his biography. He is mentioned in a handful of other publications about American Indian literature but normally plays at best a secondary role to his contemporary D'Arcy McNickle within academic discourse.

Deloria has received even less attention from academics and critics. Although this has something to do with the fact that he is still writing, it also reflects what I take to be an unfortunate prejudice among scholars against American Indian critical, as opposed to fictional, poetic, oral, or autobiographical, writings. Few scholarly studies have been written about Deloria, though he is mentioned in passing in a number of theological, anthropological, and political works. Contemporary American Indian novelists and poets, however, often draw the article- and book-length attention of scholars.

Because of this lack of definitive statements about either figure, I have attempted to provide basic reviews of their biographies and writings, while remaining focused on the overall project of addressing the issues that I have outlined. This, then, is far from a comprehensive engagement with Deloria or Mathews.

That dual task is crucial to take into account while reading what follows, because so much there is predicated on the argument that contemporary American Indian critical studies needs to address the issues outlined previously if it is to develop into a responsible and accountable discourse. Thus, those who become frustrated with sections that seem more suggestive than conclusive should understand that much of the point here is, in fact, to be convincingly suggestive rather than conclusive.

In comparing Deloria and Mathews I maintain that Native critical studies and literature have come to a point where Native critics can and should engage one another with more vigor and energy than in the past. The explosion of American Indian writing that has followed the ground-breaking reception of N. Scott Momaday and Deloria now demands sincere engagement and a willingness to ask tough questions. A guiding principle of my work, from its inception several years ago, has been to produce a book that explores the extent to which, after more than two centuries of impressive literary and critical production, critical interpretation of those writings can proceed primarily from Indian sources. I envisioned, thus, a bibliography dominated by the literature and, more important, the criticism of American Indian writers. I have tried to respect the demand that Native writers be taken seriously as critics as well as producers of literature and culture.[3]

In spite of my dissent from most aspects of contemporary critical discourse by and about American Indians, I hope readers will not see this work as a polemic against what has occurred in the past twenty-five years. Indeed, the sheer volume, quality, range, diversity, and artistry of Native American writing since 1968 is a tribute to the resiliency and resistant spirit of Native America. Twenty-five years ago, building a library of American Indian writers from books in print would have taken up no more than a few feet of shelf space. With the emergence of literally hundreds of writers since and the reprinting of many authors from before 1968, the yield now is yards and yards.

The critical issues I raise in what is still, for the most part, uncharted territory all revolve around my analysis of the ways American Indian intellectuals write about and speak to each other about the role of intellectual work in the social, political, economic, cultural, and spiritual struggle for an American Indian future. I have thought of it as being a book that I wish I could have turned to a few years ago when I was asking some of the questions herein and found few resources.

Deloria and Mathews do not specifically take up many of these issues in the works under scrutiny here. As I hope to show persuasively in this study, though, they do open up the possibility of speaking about these contemporary challenges. This study, then, examines how reading these two figures provides means through which to identify how contemporary American Indian intellectual discourse can confront the challenges of the present and the future. Having referred now several times to contemporary American Indian discourse, I will briefly outline the features within that discourse that have prompted the chapters that follow.

By the mid-1980s several distinct streams of American Indian academic criticism had appeared. The majority of people writing in these streams adhered in various ways to forms of idealism (whether liberal or radical) and essentialism. In the Fourth World formulations exemplified in the work of Ward Churchill (Creek/Cherokee Métis) and M. Annette Jaimes (Juaneño/Yaqui), the radical and polemical call to understand American Indian culture (including literature) as part of a global consciousness shared by all indigenous people in all periods of history was the central category.[4] Paula Gunn Allen (Laguna), during this same period, revisioned American Indian history to reflect a gynocentric, "solid, impregnable, ineradicable orientation toward a spirit-informed view of the universe, which provides an internal structure to both . . . consciousness and . . . art. This view is shared by all members of tribal psychic reality."[5] At their best, these streams of criticism have offered a strong counternarrative to received academic and popular understandings of American Indian people and cultures. Appeals to essentialized worldviews, though, always risk an ossifying of American Indian existence. Such a commitment to essentialized indigenous worldviews and consciousness, over the course of the decade, became a pervasive and almost requisite feature of American Indian critical writing.[6]

The dominating influence of essentialist understandings of Indian culture, of course, has been contested in various and vigorous ways. Jack Forbes (Renape/Lenape/Powhatan) and Jimmie Durham (Cherokee) have steadfastly stood by categories of analysis that highlight the material economic, social, and cultural realities that are often lost (or at least severely demoted) in essentialist discourse.[7] Katherine Shanley (Assiniboine), Chrystos (Menominee), Barbara Cameron (Lakota), and other Native women have dissented from both the essentialist feminism of Allen and the complete dismissal of Euro-American feminism of other Native women.[8] Shanley and

Kimberly Blaeser (Ojibwa) have injected contemporary literary discourse with alternatives to forms of criticism that, in the end, stereotype and parochialize American Indian writing.[9]

The strongest and most controversial critic of essentialism has been Gerald Vizenor (Ojibwa). In his fiction, poetry (including his haiku), and criticism, he has maintained a steady antiessentialist course for over two decades.[10] His early recognition of the social construction of language and racial identity further put him on the cutting edge of postmodern literature and theory. His agonistic invitation to enter the arena of independent thought, self-criticism, and creedal uncertainty make his work the most theoretically sophisticated and informed to date.

The sway of essentialism has now become less pronounced among American Indian critics. Recent work by Churchill and Jaimes, for instance, evidences less concern with worldviews than with the promotion of a "hard-line" Native political agenda and analysis of racist assumptions in American literature and political culture.[11] The emergence of the *Wicazo Sa Review*, with its gathering together of a broad range of voices in American Indian studies, has, almost by default, reoriented the discourse—for the journal's readers, at least—from its emphasis on essentialized Indians to a sincere engagement with the variety of voices and perspectives that make up contemporary Native America.

These features of contemporary American Indian critical discourse prompted the following preoccupations of this work. First and foremost, the discourse continues to evidence an avoidance of internal criticism, opting instead for a general pose of criticizing non-Indian scholarship in specific and U.S. society in general. Disputes between American Indian writers usually issue only in the strongest, most dismissive, of terms. One of many examples is Forbes's saying that the novels of Momaday and James Welch "can hardly be called political" because, according to Forbes, their novels grow out of mature capitalism's need for harmless, nostalgic fictional works.[12]

The tendency to find in the work of other American Indian writers something worthy either of unmitigated praise or of unbridled criticism stands in the way of sincere disagreement and engagement. This prevents contentious issues of, for instance, gender, sexual orientation, and economic, social, and political privilege from gaining the attention they deserve. Thus, forums in which complex critical problems of audience, reception, and representation are worked through—rather than pronouncing critical judgment—remain few and far between.

Second, few works by American Indians reveal a nuanced relationship either to the contemporary variety or to the generational history of American Indian intellectual production. To offer again one of many examples, even a text as theoretically sophisticated and concerned with local, Native critical categories as Greg Sarris's (Coast Miwok/Pomo) *Keeping Slug Woman Alive: A Holistic Approach to American Indian Texts* all but eschews references to critical writings by American Indians. Though contemporary American Indian autobiographies and novels make their way into Sarris's argument, American Indian critical work—most notably that of Vizenor, but others as well—is conspicuously absent. For example, in *Slug Woman* Sarris argues that "tradition is not fixed, but an ongoing process" and then cites someone outside of Native American discourse.[13] Twenty years and more after Deloria made this point in *God Is Red* and other places, it is striking to see how little impact American Indian critical writers have had on each other's work. The lack of historical engagement is even more pronounced, especially engagement that seeks to bring the concerns of different periods together into some kind of cohesive sense.

The third and final observation proceeds from the first two. That is, both American Indian and Native Americanist discourses continue to be preoccupied with parochial questions of identity and authenticity. Essentialist categories still reign insofar as more of the focus of scholarship has been to reduce, constrain, and contain American Indian literature and thought and to establish why something or someone is "Indian" than engage the myriad critical issues crucial to an Indian future. As Deloria says in the final chapter of *Custer Died for Your Sins*, " 'Indianness' is in the eye of the beholder."[14] Like Deloria, my concern has been to keep such questions from obscuring more pressing concerns.

By that statement I mean to highlight the unfortunate way in which contemporary discourse both by and about Indians is more interested, for instance, in the Charles Eastman (Sioux) who grew up in a traditional Sioux home than in the Charles Eastman who attended Mark Twain's seventieth birthday party or who read a paper at the First Universal Races Congress with W. E. B. Du Bois and others in 1911. As producers of American Indian literature continue to push the boundaries of creativity by bringing European vampires to Navajo country, Charlie Parker and Nat King Cole to their poems, and secular Indian lawyers to the campaign trail, criticism has remained, by and large, content with the narrowest, most parochializing foci.[15] Indeed, the inability of most contemporary criticism to speak with any clarity to the science fiction of Russell Bates (Kiowa), the mystery writing of Martin Cruz Smith (Senecu del Sur/Yaqui), the political humor of Will Rogers (Cherokee), and a host of other Indian writers whose work does not fit into standard definitions of Indian writing seems more than enough justification for some fundamental reworking of scholarly understandings of American Indian literature, culture, and experience.[16]

Deloria and Mathews provide ideal subjects for working against the grain of contemporary discourse. Both contend in their work that the success or failure of American Indian communal societies has always been predicated not upon a set of uniform, unchanging beliefs, but rather upon a commitment to the groups and the groups' futures. Further, they come from adjoining generations. Putting them side by side in a study such as this highlights both the differences and the similarities of different periods in American Indian intellectual and political history. Finally, the global perspectives and international experiences that are integral to their works give the lie to any critical strategy that would seek to reduce them to narrow, stereotypical categories and formulations.

Some of the issues this study does not cover in depth are matters that may seem to many necessary in a work of American Indian criticism. The present work is concerned primarily with American Indian creative and critical writers, and a look at the Bibliography reveals that it is dominated by references to American Indian writers. I can foresee almost countless objections to this use of sources—all of them valid at some level. I will predict a few of them and explain why I have not engaged other perspectives that some scholars may believe are necessary.

My lack of extended engagement with the social sciences will be of concern to some. It might seem audacious, for instance, to discuss Deloria's and Mathews's theories of the origin of religion without making reference to Ake Hultkrantz, Christopher Vecsey, Mircea Eliade, Clifford Geertz, Sigmund Freud, or any other non-Native who has addressed this subject. Others will find it frustrating that I have not placed Mathews in the tradition of U.S. nature writing that runs through Ralph Waldo Emerson, Henry David Thoreau, John Muir, Gifford Pinchot, Aldo Leopold, Rachel Carson, Wendell Berry, and so on. The list of excluded perspectives could go on to include the obvious parallels between Deloria and process thinkers such as Alfred North Whitehead or iconoclastic social critics such as Mark Twain, or the obvious connections between Mathews and Charles Darwin and his followers.

I have avoided discussing these relationships to social science, religious studies, and American literature, in fact, because they are obvious. In focusing tightly on Mathews, Deloria, and other Native writers I have hoped to highlight the benefits that come from reading across American Indian writings. To include a broader range of concerns would risk losing that point. I have thus experimented here with privileging neglected voices and strategies in order to draw from them fresh ways of reading Native material.

The project, therefore, is several steps removed from a full-blown American Indian criticism. This is perhaps nowhere more evident than in my use of terminology: I have consciously employed a large set of terms without defining them in detail. Categories such as sovereignty, self-determination, tribal, and process appear without much detailed specification of how I am using them. I have tried to recognize that these words are problematic in spite of continuing to carry a certain political, emotional, and critical force. This is perhaps most true of sovereignty, a term from European theological and political discourse that finally does little to describe the visions and goals of American Indian communities that seek to retain a discrete identity. To simply abandon such terms, though, risks abandoning their abiding force and utility.

The same is true of the issue of identity politics, where the influx of supposed Indian voices in academic criticism defies understanding, much less resolution and definition. Indeed, the cruel irony of so many people claiming the "right" to Native identity at the academic and creative level while racist violence and prejudice continue unabated at the local, community level is one of the many conflicts between academic discourse and community experience for which I hope to lay groundwork for discussion in this work.

I have avoided these issues mainly out of a sense that several prior questions need answering if definition in these various areas is to make critical sense. Thus, the best way of reading the following work is to keep in mind that I am laying groundwork rather than erecting structures.

Even without these issues, the study outlined so far may already seem rather bulky. To sort out the various pieces I have broken down the study into chapters that employ three modes of inquiry: intellectual history, literary criticism, and the role of American Indian intellectuals in the struggle for an American Indian future. These three modes build upon one another and are, symbiotically, an articulation and demonstration of the critical framework I have drawn out of Mathews and Deloria.

In the first chapter I have established the context of Deloria and Mathews through a critical reading of their place among American Indian intellectuals of the twentieth century. They become part of what I have styled as four important moments in the history of American Indian writing. That history shifts along the way from a one-sided discourse dominated by strong advocates for integration of American Indians into the U.S. mainstream to the present much more inclusive discourse, which takes into account neglected voices. Along with giving some sense of the biographies of Mathews and Deloria, this approach allows me to argue that the context of Native writers is the most natural and productive starting point for comparing them.

The second chapter is a literary critical discussion of Mathews's novel *Sundown*, a story that portrays the internal differences of an American Indian community. What emerges in that chapter is a method of reading *Sundown* by reading across both Mathews's and Deloria's work. I have worked to call into question readings of *Sundown* that contend that it is mired in tragedy, victimization, and hopelessness. In the method of reading that I suggest, I have argued that both figures perceive community and land as central critical categories and that American Indian ceremonial traditions should be understood as process-centered and materially based.

The third chapter draws from the previous chapters a way of envisioning the role American Indian writers can play in the struggle for American Indian sovereignty and self-determination. In it I have introduced the concept of intellectual sovereignty as an attempt to describe the perspectives of Mathews and Deloria. I move in that chapter toward a cultural criticism that is grounded in American Indian experiences but which can draw on the insights and experiences of others who have faced similar struggles.

Most readers will have recognized by now that the issues with which I am dealing here are similar to those found in many contemporary theological, feminist, and postcolonial literary critical discourses. In approaching these issues in the modal way that I have rather than with a methodology borrowed from one or more of these oppositional discourses, I have hoped to produce a study that, though it may seem overly separatist to some, accepts the influences and complexities of contemporary and historical American Indian life and prepares the ground for more fruitfully engaging non-Native critical discourses. Indeed, what follows in many ways stands or falls on how well it removes American Indian critical discourse from what I consider its essentialist, parochializing strategies and prepares for such wide-ranging engagement.

The framework I have suggested, finally, is not an attempt to define a critical discourse free from influences outside of American Indian experience. By following the path I have suggested here, though, I believe I am placing myself in the same position as every American Indian person who struggles to find a way toward a self-determined future. Along that path many sources of strength and power appear that, for whatever reason, have been mostly looked past. Deloria and Mathews, for me, have been two of those sources.

1 / Deloria and Mathews in the Context of American Indian Intellectual Traditions from 1890 to 1990

In 1978 Russell Thornton (Cherokee) told a panel of other Native scholars, "We [in American Indian studies] have no disciplinary traditions," and he was not challenged.[1] Thornton's comment, given the context of fledgling American Indian studies programs in universities around the United States, was in many ways correct. Born of a highly politicized moment less than a decade earlier, these programs had come to a point where rhetoricized demands were giving way to internal self-reflection on the benefits and dangers of the sudden presence of significant numbers of American Indian scholars and creative writers in U.S. universities.

What sort of future, Thornton and other panelists were asking, could be had by the strange collection of Native poets, novelists, social critics, academicians, radical political activists-turned-professors, and others who were fulfilling student demands for diversity on U.S. campuses? And how was their work part of American Indian community and political struggles? Would these intellectuals remain a motley collection from a variety of backgrounds and academic disciplines, brought together under an umbrella that could be taken away when soft institutional money dried up, or would they develop some approach to their various work that would set it apart from that done about American Indians in other parts of the university? In one sense, then, Thornton's remark presents with clarity the dilemma of a group that must find a way of consolidating power in a new, potentially beneficial situation.

1

Since Thornton made his comment, much has changed in the field of American Indian studies. The body of literary, critical, and academic work that has emerged is remarkable. Along with the arrival of many new, contemporary voices, numerous books from the earlier part of the century and before either have made it into print for the first time or have been reprinted. The period during which Thornton made his comment was one in which scholars and writers were, in a sense, filling in the descriptive gaps and providing broad overviews of American Indian literary, historical, and cultural studies focused mainly on oral traditions; the present moment, in contrast, more fully offers the possibility of understanding contemporary intellectual production in the context of over two centuries of a written, Native intellectual tradition. In this way American Indian intellectual discourse can now ground itself in its own history the way that African-American, feminist, and other oppositional discourses have.[2]

In this chapter I will discuss what happens when we recognize that, although we may have no immediately accessible tradition that informs us how to confront present challenges, we do have many examples of Native writers and scholars who have confronted similar situations. When we take that tradition seriously, I will argue, we empower our work. First, we see that, far from engaging in some new and novel practice that belongs necessarily to the process of assimilating and enculturating non-Native values, we are doing something that Natives have done for hundreds of years—something that can be and has been an important part of resistance to assimilation and survival. Such a generational view, as I hope will emerge from this discussion, provides a new historical and critical site that invites us to see contemporary work as belonging to a process centuries long, rather than decades long, of engaging the future contours of Indian America. Second, we stand on firmer ground in our interlocutorial role with Eurocentric scholarly theories and categories, whose methodologies and disciplinary traditions too often become monoliths to be either copied uncritically or made into bugbears that are engaged in an endless dance of criticism and dependence. Third, critically reading our own tradition allows us to see some of the mistakes of the past as we analyze the problems of the present. This, of course, requires that interpreting the Native tradition be critical rather than hagiographic. Finally, and perhaps most important, reading critically our own tradition is a matter of respect—the same sort of respect we would like to be accorded by future generations.

I have conducted my comparison of John Joseph Mathews and Vine Deloria Jr. in the context of this tradition; in this chapter I discuss their place within Native intellectual history of the past one hundred years. My effort here is to provide a critical approach to and an example of working within their part of the Native tradition—those public and academic figures whose work is primarily, though not exclusively, concerned with reaching non-Native audiences.[3] Further, rather than focusing on a particular genre, I have included here the greatest possible range of Native public writing. Though this strategy leaves open questions of literary quality and generic hierarchy, it offers a wide, diverse pool of writers and texts.[4] It also recognizes that much of the best and most interesting Native writing has not issued in forms that are easy to categorize.

In doing so I have understood Mathews and Deloria as being part of four important moments for Native public intellectuals between 1890 and the present. Without drawing lines and borders too strongly around them, I will argue in this chapter that the past century has featured two periods (1890-1925 and 1961-1973) in which Native writers associated closely with one another, and two other periods (1925-1961 and 1973 to the present) marked by a lack of associative cohesion. Though using such a marked periodization might undercut the sense of heterogeneity I hope to demonstrate, these historical moments provide a way of at least provisionally understanding the sweep of the past one hundred years. The story here, then, is one that highlights the political commitments and associations among Native writers rather than focusing only on a history of their ideas.

Beginning this discussion at the end of the nineteenth century is by no means to suggest that what happened before then is less interesting. Native written intellectual tradition reaches back at least to Samson Occom's (Mohegan) missionary writings in the 1700s and includes other missionary figures such as William Apess (Pequot) and William Jones (Ojibwa); lecturers and activists such as Sarah Winnemucca Hopkins (Paiute) and Susette LaFlesche (Omaha); the

Cherokee intellectuals John Ross, John Rollin Ridge, and Elias Bou-
dinot; scores of journalists, such as Alexander Posey (Creek), who
worked for Native-run, English, and Native-language newspapers;
historical and political writers such as George Copway (Ojibwa)
and Simon Pokagon (Potawotamie); and several men and women
whose fictional work appeared in periodicals such as *Harper's Magazine* and *Atlantic Monthly* in the latter half of the nineteenth
century.

The work of transitional figures whose writing in many ways prepared the ground for those who emerged at the turn of the century
also belongs to this incomplete list. They include E. Pauline
Johnson (Mohawk), Sophia Alice Callahan (Creek), Francis La-
Flesche (Omaha), and George Bushotter (Dakota). Though many of
these writers continued working well into the twentieth century, this
study begins with the generation that emerged after the Wounded
Knee Massacre of 1890.[5]

That period, as I will argue in this chapter, is important because
it marks the first coming together of a generation of Native writers
into common, or at least similar, political projects. That coming
together starts with the Christian and secular assimilationist writing
of Charles Eastman [Ohiyesa] (Sioux), Carlos Montezuma [Wassaja]
(Yavapai), Gertrude Simmons Bonnin [Zitkala-Sa] (Sioux), and
other members of the Society of American Indians.

This chapter, then, is not so much concerned with a comprehensive reading of North American Native intellectual history as it is
with initiating discussion of what this earlier discourse tells us about
more contemporary intellectual challenges. The past three decades,
in my reading of the tradition, are important not simply for the in-
crease in production of Native writing, but because they represent a
significant shift in the diversity and experiences represented in Native intellectual discourse. That discourse, as I have styled it, has
been tremendously one-sided, favoring the most moderate, coopera-
tionist voices. This contemporary moment, I will argue, is the first
one in which advocates for community-based renewal have had wide
access to Native written discourse. Also, historically silent voices
from a full, diverse range of contemporary American Indian experience have begun to occupy a place within Native discourse.

Advocacy for a traditionalist-nationalist vision for the first time in the midst of a tradition that is otherwise dominated by Christian converts and thoroughgoing secularists is perhaps the most important feature of this shift in the discourse. The concomitant emergence of the voices of poor and urban Natives extremely alienated from tradition, gay and lesbian Natives who face persecution and discrimination in their own communities, women with a feminist or woman-centered critical analysis, and other doubly and triply marginated voices is also of critical importance in the shift of the past twenty years.

1890-1916: Assimilationism and Apocalypticism

Less than a week after announcing his engagement to transplanted Bostonian Elaine Goodale, Sioux physician Charles Eastman (Ohiyesa) stood defending the Pine Ridge Indian Agency against a group of Oglala Lakota ghost dancers who had learned of the massacre of over three hundred Minneconjou Lakotas eleven miles away at Wounded Knee Creek on December 29, 1890. Eastman, after being presented to the Lake Mohonk Conference as a model for what assimilationist education could produce, had arrived at Pine Ridge in November to practice medicine among his own people and to help them adjust to the white world that surrounded them.[6] He was, however, immediately caught up in trying to avert an armed uprising.[7]

Three days later, after successfully defending the U.S. government agency from attack, Eastman accompanied the party in charge of burying the massacred dead and attending to any wounded that had survived in the bitter cold and wind.[8] After Wounded Knee, the Ghost Dance movement quickly faded and the peyote movement swept through Indian country. Eastman left Pine Ridge in 1892 and went on to become the most influential American Indian writer of his time.

Eastman was one of many educated middle-class American Indians who worked to "civilize" their Native brothers and sisters through the Society of American Indians (SAI), the federal government, and white-dominated friend-of-the-Indian groups. The Society of American Indians, founded in 1911, drew its constituency from the university-trained economic elite of eastern Native groups, mixed-blood reservation families, assimilated Native families who had lost all but nominal ties to Native culture, Christian converts who had attended seminaries, orphaned Natives who had been adopted and raised by white families, and, most important, graduates of and other Natives connected to Richard Henry Pratt's Carlisle Indian Industrial School.[9]

The coming together of these figures marks the first time Native intellectuals had joined in a common organization. Carlisle and its progeny were the educational arm of federal policy that during that time was concerned with individually allotting communally held Native lands, abrogating traditional forms of government, and undermining all efforts to maintain community integrity. It and other off-reservation schools that followed its program of disallowing Native dress, language, and religion produced the generation that supported the assimilationist ideology that followed Wounded Knee. Pratt, whose program of educational reform began with Indian prisoners held captive in Fort Marion in the 1870s, had as his slogan "Kill the Indian and save the man!"[10] Eastman was for a time the "outings officer" at Carlisle, and Dr. Carlos Montezuma (Wassaja) was staff physician.[11] The work of both important figures bears the mark of Pratt's influence. Richard Sanderville (Blackfeet), though not as well known as others, was a product of Carlisle and returned to his Blackfeet people to work for the U.S. government both as an interpreter and as an anthropological informer.[12] Angel Decora (Winnebago) and Sioux writer Gertrude Simmons Bonnin (Zitkala-Sa) went to school elsewhere but taught for Pratt in the early part of this century.[13]

At a founding meeting of the society twenty-one years after Wounded Knee, Eastman commented, "In connection with the words of the last speaker, that there has been a great deal of injustice done to our tribes, I wish to say that really no prejudice has existed so far as the American Indian is concerned."[14] Whether Eastman was suffering from a lapse of memory or honestly believed that the history of Native to non-Native relationships of his time had nothing to do with prejudice, this story points with some clarity to the quite scandalous treatment of American Indian people during the period, on the one hand, and the blinding progressivistic optimism of Eastman and other intellectuals toward such treatment on the other.

This generation was the integrationist legacy of post-Wounded Knee existence. They were adults at the time of the transition to reservation life, the federal allotment policy, and the land and lease swindles that came along with allotment and western expansion. Faced with the prospect of total dispossession if Natives continued to resist the U.S. government, these figures believed strongly in doing away with special educational and health programs for Natives, abandonment of Native traditional government structures, and full participation in mainstream U.S. life.[15] The general intent of Carlisle and other eastern boarding schools was to turn young Natives against the traditions of their communities by any means necessary, including beatings and forced separation from family.[16]

The problem they ran into as they advocated joining with the U.S. mainstream was that the values they sought to imitate existed mainly as ideals rather than actualities. As Vine Deloria would later argue,

> The real exile of the tribes occurred with . . . the failure or inability of white society to offer a sensible and cohesive alternative to the traditions which Indians remembered. . . . The new ways which they were expected to learn were in a constant state of change because they were not a cohesive view of the world but simply adjustments which whites were making to the technology they were inventing.
>
> Had whites been able to maintain a sense of stability in their own society, which Indians had been admonished to imitate, the tribes might have been able to observe the integrity of the new way of life and make a successful transition to it. But the only alternative that white society had to offer was a chaotic and extreme individualism.[17]

Thus, on Deloria's reading of the general situation, these figures failed to recognize that the ideals they sought for U.S. society and Natives were far from realizable and that the Indian situation at the turn of the century was a battle of community values versus individualistic chaos rather than a battle of one set of cohesive, livable values against another.

Most of these figures eventually rejected Pratt's paternalism, but they stood by his belief that Natives must internalize the ideals of Anglo-American civil society.[18] They were at the same time committed to preserving the memory of tribal life and maintaining what they saw as the laudable values of traditional life, such as honesty and family responsibility. Such preservation, of course, took place only in the context of attempting to live out the ideals of white Western civilization. Carlos Montezuma was perhaps the most radical among these Progressives, believing not only that Native people could match whites in living out mainstream values, but that Natives were in fact superior and would prove as much if only the "barriers" of Indian schools, languages, and reservations were removed.[19] The Apache doctor said in one of his editorials for his newspaper, "The Indian Bureau is all bosh, a bunk, the greatest humbug. To do the greatest good for the Indian race by Congress is to abolish the Indian Bureau."[20]

Though their work ranges in genre from Bonnin's fiction and essays to Eastman's memoirs of his childhood to the high polemics of Montezuma's journalism, all of it issues from similar political commitments and affiliations. Eastman's memoirs, for instance, are highly sentimental accounts of his childhood in which he portrays Natives as needy for, worthy of, and ready for inclusion in mainstream civilization.[21] The purpose of these authors, continuous with their SAI politics, was to gain sympathy from white audiences for the difficult, but to the authors necessary, process of becoming American citizens.[22] Their appeal in this work, coterminous with the liberal and progressive politics of their time, was for non-Natives to act with justice and honor as Natives underwent this process.

However troubling we might find the SAI generation's support for and advancement of the policies of the U.S. government, we cannot fault their sincerity or their commitment to and love for American Indian people. Simply to label them misguided, brainwashed, self-hating collaborators, in other words, misses the point of their achievement. This is not to suggest that we allow their sincerity to blind us to the perturbing implications of their work, which provides a means of asking difficult ethical, cultural, and political questions in the context of complex, often dire, situations.

A good illustration comes from recent attempts to interpret the work of Bonnin. William Willard (Cherokee) has written about her twice in the Indian-founded and -edited *Wicazo Sa Review*, in 1985 and in 1991. Willard gives the 1985 essay the title "Zitkala-Sa: A Woman Who Would Be Heard." He focuses in it on Bonnin's four decades of tireless efforts as an educator, lobbyist, editor of the SAI's journal, and writer of short fiction and portrays her life as an example for contemporary activists. Willard says of her, "She left a legacy of activism for future generations of Indian leaders."[23]

He bases this sympathetic evaluation on her lobbying and investigative efforts regarding, among other topics, abuses in the Bureau of Indian Affairs, land and water rights, and irresponsible management of Oklahoma Indian oil resources. Another positive evaluation of Bonnin, along with Montezuma and Eastman, comes from Paula Gunn Allen. Writing that "the measures favored by white liberals did nothing" to alleviate problems for Natives, she says, "the situation improved when Native people themselves became involved," and includes Bonnin in her list of those Natives. M. Annette Jaimes (Juaneño-Yaqui), and Theresa Halsey (Standing Rock Sioux) also point to Bonnin as a strong branch in their genealogy of strong Indian women writers/activists.[24]

Not to point out the obvious positive contributions of Bonnin and others in telling the story of early-twentieth-century Native America would be to omit a major part of the historical record, an omission committed by most historians who write about the period.[25] To react to that omission with uncritical praise of these figures, though, is just as major an error. More important, such praise obscures the serious questions these figures raise about contemporary work.

Willard takes this up when writing about another subject in which Bonnin figured prominently. His 1991 essay "The First Amendment, Anglo-Conformity and American Indian Religious Freedom" looks at the suppression of peyotism and other Native religions. He blames "white supremacy" for being the driving force behind efforts to make illegal the use of peyote in religious ceremonies.[26] Any us-versus-them rhetoric he might have been tempted to use, though, was made difficult by the presence of Bonnin and other SAI figures in the antipeyote camp.[27]

Given these Natives' staunch and energetic support of the anti-peyote campaign, Willard earnestly presents the way their influence hindered the efforts of those who were seeking to have the U.S. Congress pass legislation to protect the religious freedom of American Indians. He shows how Bonnin and her Native husband used the fact that they were themselves Natives to lend authority to their positions regarding peyote. Willard, further, does not overstate the importance of friend-of-the-Indian groups that lobbied for religious freedom. Rather, he is careful to point out those Native organizations, such as the All-Pueblo Council and the newly organized Native American Church, that were instrumental in protecting their own religious freedom.[28]

In approaching his subject this way Willard confronts himself with other important facts about Bonnin. He speaks of her critique of Pratt and the boarding-school ideology that she had supported. Far from being brainwashed, she shows herself to be opposed to the paternalism of Pratt and other non-Native educators, but she remained an opponent of peyote and other forms of Native existence.

Bonnin's opposition to peyote is but one example of how reading our own tradition critically can be more honest and less celebratory. Eastman, Montezuma, and others provide case studies just as interesting and complex. The simple point here is that understanding the literary output of the period requires an acknowledgment of how closely the authors related to each other politically and how much the work they produced was guided by the political landscape they inhabited. They corresponded with one another, attended the same meetings, sometimes collaborated, and Montezuma and Bonnin were even engaged to be married.[29] Then, as now, the background of intellectual production was specific political situations and programs.

The important points for this present study are, first, that the establishment of SAI and the interactions of the writers who emerged during this period represent the first coming together of Native intellectuals in a specific political project and, second, that their various writings are connected in content and context through their associations with one another.[30] Though they disagreed so strongly on some points, especially the antipeyote campaign, that the organization lost its fervor in the early 1920s, their disagreements were over how to accomplish the political tasks upon which they all generally agreed.[31]

The Society of American Indians, to be fair, invited those who adhered to a treaty-based, nationalist vision to their meetings and published their speeches, but "consign[ed] all those with whom it disagreed to outer darkness as traitors to the race."[32] These "traitors to the race," unfortunately, did not produce an organization or intellectuals that could create a written ideology for their traditionalist-nationalist stance. In this, American Indian intellectual history is markedly different from that, for instance, of African-Americans, who have produced political organizations that have countered with forms of black nationalism the dominant ideologies of integration (e.g., Martin Delany and Frederick Douglass, Malcolm X and Martin Luther King Jr.). However skewed this history might be in favor of the integrationist position, the written documents of these political and intellectual conflicts remain available.[33]

For American Indians, organized nationalist, noncooperationist political resistance came primarily in the form of religious movements that did not produce books, publish newspapers, or create national organizations. Before Wounded Knee these movements were activist, usually attempted to create military unity against encroaching white settlers, and often involved a prophet or messiah figure. The Native unity effort of Tecumseh and his brother, the Shawnee Prophet, in the first two decades of the nineteenth century and the Ghost Dance movement, mentioned earlier, were the last of these prophet-based unity movements.[34]

Far from what Eastman saw as a lack of prejudice against Natives, non-Native reaction to the Ghost Dance movement, both in its original nonviolent form and in its South Dakota offshoot that threatened armed struggle, sent a message to all American Indian people that any attempt at unity and protection of tradition, language, culture, religion, and political integrity would be met with violence and repressive legislation from Washington. Federal policy, fueled by Manifest Destiny ideology, dictated the repression of militant Native unity and the undermining of the integrity of American Indian people and nations.[35]

Following the rapid decline of the Ghost Dance movement after the Wounded Knee Massacre, many of the apocalypticists turned to peyotism and the soon-to-be-institutionalized Native American Church. Peyotism combines Christian symbols, American Indian spiritual practice, and the ceremonial use of hallucinogenic peyote. The society, friend-of-the-Indian groups, and members of the U.S. Congress subjected the followers of peyotism to several campaigns that sought to outlaw peyote use, part of a history of repression that continues to the present day. Yet the groups that would later become the Native American Church managed to accomplish what the U.S. government was unwilling to allow politically and culturally: internal, self-determined adaptation to a new situation.[36]

People who maintained traditional ceremonies, language, and culture make up the other important component of those who refused to cooperate with the U.S. government during this period. Christian missionaries successfully lobbied the U.S. Congress in the 1880s to suppress Native ceremonies, especially those involving any form of what they saw as self-deprivation or self-torture, and those who maintained these traditions did so often away from the scrutiny of government agents and missionaries.[37] Isolation, however, kept most of these people, except for some who ran tribal newspapers, from producing an accessible written literature.[38]

The attitude of SAI toward such traditionalist Natives was antagonistic at worst and paternalistic at best.[39] While the U.S. government was promoting the sale of Native land to settlers and acquiescing in the pervasive violence and financial swindles against Natives in many areas, SAI retained its conciliatory tone, stating in 1916 that the society was "more conscious than ever of the complex situation in which a kindly and benevolent Government has placed the Indian of the United States." The society opposed freedom of religion for Natives, especially regarding the use of peyote, and remained opposed to any strategy that would, in Montezuma's words, "keep us Indians, in making us prolong our Indian life."[40]

As the actualities of federal policy unfolded on reservations around the country, the noncooperationists were vindicated, and the middle-class intellectuals' strategy was shown to be impractical.[41] Though many American Indian people accepted the onus of making quick adjustment to the become-civilized-Christians-or-starve policies of the U.S. government, the government proved itself unwilling and unable to protect the land and resources of American Indian groups.

Importantly, rather than having accountability toward constituencies in local American Indian communities as its main priority, SAI aimed most of its work at its supporters from the many white reform organizations, such as the Women's National Indian Association, the Indian Rights Association, and the Lake Mohonk Conference, that shared the society's assimilation-with-justice goals. The Improved Order of Red Men, which sought to imitate American Indian values (but which barred Natives from membership), and other white-primitivist groups that appropriated American Indian symbols and traditions also helped create a market for books and articles about Native traditions and lifeways by SAI authors.[42]

This strong, predominantly romantic, support from white organizations concomitantly created a strong anti-African-American ideology among many SAI members, including Francis Red Fox St. James and Arthur C. Parker (Seneca).[43] In espousing a European-immigrant model for Native assimilation, Parker contended that African-Americans could not follow the same model because "the African negro was a savage who was cruel to his own race and superstitious in the extreme." Rather than becoming enlightened through their ability to reason, as Parker would have it for Natives, African-Americans could integrate only because of their "natural servility and imitativeness," which is "evidence of feeble character and inferiority."[44]

Thus, in playing into U.S. fascination with this continent's Native past and trying to corner the market on white sympathies, the public intellectuals of the turn of the century distanced themselves from the largest oppressed racial group in the United States. Any coalescing that went on between the groups was done indirectly through white intermediaries who were "friends to both" African-Americans and Natives.[45]

By 1918 the weaknesses of progressive U.S. federal policy had become apparent even to the Society of American Indians, and "the Society now had a different tone, more romantic, less rational; at once committed to instant solutions but at the same time less confident of the country's capacity to offer any solutions; more sentimental about Indian life and less closely in touch with it." Within

five years those within SAI who still supported mainstreaming ideology did so in the midst of a growing movement of white reformers
and government agents who could no longer blind themselves to the
violence and oppression of federal Indian policy. The reform groups
began casting about for a way to preserve tribal identities and pro-
mote nonpaternalistic self-government. After successfully lobbying
for the passage of the Indian Citizenship Act of 1924, SAI never
again played a major role in national politics.[46]

Before the passage of the act, Montezuma came down with tu-
berculosis and prepared to die. He traveled to the Fort McDowell
Yavapai Reservation and lived out his days in a "brush shelter built
in the style of pre-reservation camps."[47]

The first important moment of twentieth-century American Indian intellectual history thus came to an end. After decades of promoting the Indian cause in print, through public events at which he
would wear traditional dress, and in official government capacities,
Charles Eastman spent the last years of his life, separated from
Elaine Goodale Eastman, fishing and hunting in Canada.[48] Somewhat like Montezuma, he died in 1939 while living in a tepee at a
primitivist camp outside of Detroit.[49]

1925-1960: John Joseph Mathews and
a Generation of Free Agents

While the post-Pratt generation of SAI intellectuals was putting the
best face on the violent realities that the integrationist project was
producing in American Indian communities, the next generation of
Native intellectual figures was growing up in the midst of them. The
period between the demise of the Society of American Indians and
the emergence of the National Congress of American Indians in
1944 produced a significant number of Native intellectuals; but
without the presence of a national organization or a coherent political project, the work of these intellectuals has no common theme
except in the few years during which the movement toward John
Collier's Indian Reorganization Act under President Franklin
Roosevelt provided something of a focal point.[50]

Because this is the period during which John Joseph Mathews began his writing career, I will structure my remarks about this generation around him. His enigmatic biography is one of many in a generation that did not have a common experience such as the Carlisle School to make any one of them a typical example. Theirs was a generation made up of individuals whose individual projects reflect the time in which they worked.

Mathews was born in 1894 in the period before the Osage Reservation was allotted and became a county of the state of Oklahoma. Of the Native intellectuals in his time he went on to become the most cosmopolitan, most philosophical, and most suspicious of Euro-American values. Though he recognized, perhaps even more profoundly than the post-Pratt generation, the need for American Indian people to make radical adjustments to colonization, his critical stance toward the values and underpinnings of Euro-American culture set him apart from them.

Mathews's bicultural existence as a youngster did not fit into any of the typical patterns of reservation life at the time.[51] Three groups dominated the political and social scene of Osage life throughout his early years. The "full-blood" group represented those still connected to the "intermeshed politicoreligious system" of clans and ceremonies.[52] This group had long been the majority in postcontact political dealings with the U.S. government, but by the turn of the century their influence was declining.[53]

The second important group, the "mixed-blood" faction, had been a factor in Osage politics since at least the early 1800s, but with the final move to the Oklahoma reservation they "took advantage of their bicultural heritage to use the conflict between the races for their own economic advantage."[54] This group, often the product of liaisons between French Catholic male interlopers and widowed Osage women, has frequently been a focal point of mistrust from members of the most nationalist of full-blood families, even though Osage destiny has for a century been wrapped up with them. By Mathews's time, however, some from the full-blood group had joined with the mixed-bloods to make up the pro-allotment Progressive faction.

The third important group in Mathews's early milieu was made up of the many white settlers, ranchers, and traders who were attracted to the wealth enjoyed by Osages as leasers of vast rangeland

and later as communal owners of one of the continent's largest oil-fields. Some of these white men, especially those who were married to Osage women, manipulated themselves onto the tribal rolls in order to share in Osage wealth.[55]

Though most often identified with the mixed-bloods, Mathews in fact does not belong properly to any of these groups.[56] His father, William Mathews, came from an English Protestant, rather than a French Catholic, family that had traded among the Osages for several generations. Mathews's great-grandfather, William Shirley Mathews, married A-Ci'n-Ge, an Osage woman.[57] However, because the Mathews lineage is traced to an Osage woman and Osages are patrilineal, Mathews did not fit into the full-blood faction, either. His associations with all groups were thus somewhat tenuous, and he belonged, finally, to none of them.

Because his father was a successful trader and drew money from Osage range, then oil, leases, Mathews grew up in the midst of wealth. He lived as a child in a large house on Agency Hill, the focal point then and now of Osage relations with the U.S. government. From that house he could see Bird Creek and the small western town of Pawhuska growing beside it. In the other direction he could see and hear the village where many traditional Osages lived in spite of being able to afford modern houses.[58]

Though his early life was dominated by the trappings of non-Native culture, Mathews maintained constant contact with traditional Osage people during his childhood. Speaking of what he saw and heard from that house, Mathews says in the introduction to his 1961 tribal history *The Osages*, "I was a very small boy when the seed which was to disturb me all of my life was planted. . . . There floated up to my room through the open window . . . a long, drawn-out chant broken by weeping."[59] He was hearing the traditional chanting at dawn of an Osage band camped near his house, the same Big Hills band, in fact, from which his great-grandmother had come.

At about the time Mathews became conscious of such chanting, Osages were embroiled in a political dispute that continues to this day. Because the U.S. government was intent on quick acculturation and allotment of all Native groups, it worked actively to undermine all Osage efforts to retain tribal sovereignty and communal integrity.

This, importantly, was the driving force of federal policy during the period—individualizing communally held lands and abrogating relationships with self-determined tribal governments.[60]

In 1897 the Osage full-blood faction was unsuccessful in having names of non-Osages purged from tribal rolls, because the U.S. government found in them the swing votes it needed to gain the "consent" of the Osage Nation in allotment and other policies. In 1898 the U.S. government unilaterally proclaimed that as of April 1, 1900, it would no longer recognize the authority of the Osage National Council, a representative governmental body that Osages had founded in 1880 on the model of the neighboring Cherokee's constitutional government. In 1904 Osages voted for allotment.[61]

Between 1906 and 1908 the federal government established the tribal roll, John Joseph Mathews being on it, and allotted the reservation equally among all those enrolled. Osages had carefully made provision, though, that only the surface of the reservation would be allotted, reserving all mineral rights for the original allottees and their descendants. In both of these provisions—that all reservation land be allotted and that subsurface rights remain in communal ownership—Osages were unique among allotted Native groups.[62]

Because of the shared oil and mineral holdings, the already prosperous Osages came into major wealth, somewhat as present-day Kuwait and other small Persian Gulf countries have done. Mathews calls the period from 1916 until the Great Depression "The Great Frenzy."[63] This is the time during which he came of age.

In his family's house on Agency Hill Mathews had servants and fine furnishings. His life was a combination of upper-class luxury and contact with traditional Osage culture. He spent his youth hunting on horseback around the Osage prairie, reading books of American and European literature, and listening to the stories of older Osages in the villages. He watched firsthand the ascendancy of peyotism as the dominant form of religious life among the traditional Osages.[64]

When Mathews left Osage County for the University of Oklahoma in 1914, he left a situation in which many mixed-bloods and other Progressives were attempting to build fortunes with the money they were receiving each quarter. They were by and large unequipped for competing with the many white businesspeople who arrived at the same time to take advantage of Osage wealth.[65]

The period between 1916 and 1924 saw the apex of oil wealth, the onset of criminal activity by white residents of the county designed to separate Osages from their wealth, and the acquiescence of the federal government in the plunder. The U.S. government placed Osage money in the trusteeship of non-Native "guardians" who often were unscrupulous in their fiduciary responsibility. Through these guardianships and various leasing scams many Osages lost the land that had been allotted in 1906. The most famous scheme came during what newspapers of the time called the "Osage Reign of Terror," in which a white man married an Osage woman and systematically conspired to inherit several shares of Osage oil wealth through murdering members of her family over a number of years.[66]

These events took place by and large while Mathews was abroad, and only upon his return did he understand the great changes brought about by more than two decades of spectacular wealth. At the University of Oklahoma he was a football player and a fraternity member. In his senior year he interrupted his education and joined the U.S. Calvary in World War I. His superior night vision and leadership ability, however, soon made him a prime candidate for pilot training, and he finished out his time in the service as a pilot in the U.S. Signal Corps. Afterward, he returned to the university and received a degree in geology in 1920.[67]

In 1921 Mathews was offered a Rhodes Scholarship to attend Oxford University, but he thought the scholarship too restrictive and decided to attend Oxford a year later, with his own money. He was graduated B.A. Oxon with a degree in natural sciences in 1923. After Oxford Mathews attended the School for International Affairs in Geneva and was a League of Nations correspondent for the *Philadelphia Ledger*. He also traveled extensively in Europe, North Africa, and the Middle East. During a hunting trip in North Africa in 1928 Mathews had an experience that would forever change his life.[68]

While he was camping one night, a band of bedouins on horseback surrounded Mathews's camp and began firing their weapons into the air. Mathews said of the incident:

I remember very distinctly one evening, when we were preparing our meal, suddenly it came to my guide and my cook
that it was time to worship. So they fell on their knees, faces
toward Mecca, as usual. In this situation you feel so clumsy so
out of things—you feel that you are an absolutely sinful person. About this time some Kabyles, a wild tribe of Arabs, came
up who were not Mohammedan and had not known religion
at all—wild! They came across the sand. I think there were
about six or eight of them firing their Winchesters, the model
1894 lever. I thought, here, we're in trouble. My guide and my
cook were prostrate. They surrounded us shooting all the
way—on their Arab horses—all mares, incidentally. Then they
got off and ate with us. They were very friendly.

That night I got to thinking about it, and I thought that's
exactly what happened to me one day when I was a little boy,
riding on the Osage prairies. Osage warriors with only their
breechclouts and their guns had come up and surrounded
us—firing. Of course, I knew some of them, about them; they
knew me, who I was. That's what we called joy shooting, you
see, just joy. So, I got homesick, and I thought, what am I doing over here? Why don't I go back and take some interest in
my people? Why not go back to the Osages? They've got culture. So, I came back.[69]

This single event, as Mathews saw it, drew him back from the extensive wanderings he had engaged in since leaving for college. In
his references to the model of the rifle and in the observation that all
of the horses were mares, Mathews reveals his keen memory for rus-
tic detail. However, in recounting this story fifty years later
Mathews did not state that before his return to Pawhuska he first
lived in Los Angeles, sold real estate, and had a marriage of "short
duration."[70]

Mathews's return to the United States and his talent for writing
converged with a new concern for Indian affairs. Gertrude Bonnin
was one of the few figures from the Society of American Indians to
remain on the scene during this time. She had begun moving away
from the politics of SAI as early as the antipeyote campaign, which
had occurred during the second decade of the century.[71]

Increasingly, Bonnin linked her efforts to the reform movement
whose leader was John Collier. Visiting the Pueblos, he "found in

the Pueblo communal and ceremonial life an answer to the problems of human society . . . and . . . eagerly joined" the Indian reform movement.[72] Less than a decade later Collier became Franklin Roosevelt's Indian commissioner and pursued through legislation and federal programs a rescue of Native communities, which he called the "Red Atlantis."[73]

Because of political compromise and hostile reaction among some Native groups and individuals, Collier did not realize his utopian hope of reviving communal ceremonial and political life among Natives. The U.S. Congress moderated many of his Indian Reorganization Act's most important provisions, such as the reestablishment of Native land bases through compulsory return of lost lands. Further, the U.S. government did not back Collier's program with enough money to make most of its provisions sufficiently operable.[74] The act remains a turning point, though, insofar as it reversed the assimilation policy and ended statutory persecution of most Native religious ceremonies.[75]

Though Bonnin eventually parted company with Collier's politics, she for many years supported his goals. She had moved so completely into this protribal position that in 1926 she founded a new organization, the National Council of American Indians, hoping to bridge the gap between the professional, educated middle-class roots of SAI and grassroots Native leadership in American Indian communities around the country. She achieved neither, as "the tribes to whom Mrs. Bonnin addressed her appeals did not respond, and the educated Indian elite took no interest in Mrs. Bonnin's work."[76] With SAI not functioning, however, the National Council was the only national Native organization in the United States until the founding of the National Congress of American Indians in 1944.[77]

With only spotty Native support, Bonnin linked her efforts with the work of groups such as the General Federation of Women's Clubs and the Indian Rights Association. She edited the National Council's *Indian Newsletter* until her death in 1938.[78] Others from SAI either retired from active political work or became involved in what Hertzberg calls "fraternal" Native organizations.[79] The time was ripe for a new generation of Native writers.

It was in this situation that Mathews began his literary career. The small flurry of works by him and other Native writers that came out in the late 1920s and early 1930s reflects the growing sentiment in U.S. political circles for a reform of federal Indian policy and provided fuel for this growing, white-dominated, reform movement.[80] Writers from this period, however, were not the products of Carlisle-style education; they had grown up on reservations with the day-to-day realities of violence and dispossession that SAI had so successfully ignored.

Setting the stage for the emergence of these writers were, among others, John Milton Oskison and Will Rogers, both Cherokees born in Indian Territory. Oskison attended Stanford and Harvard, played a somewhat peripheral role in SAI, and went on to become a successful magazine editor at *Collier's*. He wrote several novels about the American Southwest, all of which feature some Indian characters. Though an explicit concern for Indian social and political issues is not central to his work in the 1920s, his career has as bookends works that deal with Indian issues.[81]

Rogers's vaudeville entertainment, newspaper columns, speeches, and other writings brought an Indian presence into the consciousness of many Americans. Though Rogers is not normally accorded an important place within Native literary history, because Indian issues were not the preoccupation of his work, his vast popularity was at least in part magnified by his Native identity.[82]

D'Arcy McNickle (Cree Métis), enrolled as a member of the Confederated Salish and Kutenai Tribes, has received the most critical attention of those American Indian writers who emerged immediately before and during the Great Depression and the New Deal. Born in 1904 on the Flathead Reservation in Montana, McNickle studied at the University of Montana from 1921 to 1925, then at Oxford University for one academic year in 1925-1926.[83] Following his return from England McNickle never again resided on a long-term basis in a Native community. He first lived in New York City, trying to establish himself as a writer. In 1934 he reclaimed his Native identity and began working as an increasingly important member of Collier's staff at the Bureau of Indian Affairs. He was also a cofounder of the National Congress and produced several works of history and political theory, along with his fiction.[84]

The written works of McNickle, Salishan novelist Mourning Dove (a.k.a. Christine Quintasket), and Mathews portrayed the realities Indian people had faced in the years following allotment. The change in public opinion that produced a market for these works rather than sentimental stories like those of Eastman is exemplified by the history of Mourning Dove's *Cogewea: The Half-Blood*.[85] She completed the novel in 1916, when assimilationism was still the dominant ideology in Indian affairs, but it was not published until eleven years later, when the mood was changing to reform.

Mourning Dove lacked the level of education and training of Mathews and McNickle, making the story she (and her editors) wrote one that she could connect with more easily than other contemporary writers.[86] Unfortunately, because of this lack of education and the story's jarring editing, the novel is difficult in both its language and its style. Neither it nor her collection of Okanogan tales, *Coyote Stories*, was a financial success, and she remained an obscure figure until the republication of *Cogewea* in 1981.[87] When she died in 1938, her contribution to American Indian intellectual history was still more than forty years from wide recognition.[88]

McNickle's *The Surrounded* also found only a limited readership at the time of its publication, but it remains the most widely read and studied American Indian work from the period before N. Scott Momaday.[89]

Mathews, unlike his contemporaries, made an immediate impact with his first book. Mathews's 1932 history of reservation transition, *Wah'Kon-Tah: The Osage and the White Man's Road*, was a phenomenal success and was chosen as a featured selection of the Book-of-the-Month Club. *Wah'Kon-Tah* came about somewhat fortuitously when, almost immediately upon his return to the Osage, Mathews received in an estate the journal of Laban Miles, who had worked as an Indian agent among the Osage during the reservation transitional period. At the prompting of University of Oklahoma Press editor Joseph Brandt, Mathews rewrote the journal into a historical novel of the period. The resulting book was a fabulous success, expecially considering the deepening Great Depression. The Book-of-the-Month Club's selection of it made it the first book by an American Indian and the first university press book ever to be so chosen. When Mathews traveled to New York for a series of receptions and cocktail parties, publishing houses besieged him with contract offers for another book.[90]

Mathews followed up *Wah' Kon-Tah* in 1934 with a novel, *Sundown*, but it did not have the same critical or popular success.[91] With the passage of the Indian Reorganization Act in 1934, the deepening depression, and the advent of World War II, neither Mathews nor any other Native writer would enjoy much critical success for the next thirty years. It was at this time that Mathews moved from Pawhuska to a small sandstone house on his allotment land eight miles from town. He named the house "The Blackjacks" after the running scrub oak that dominates the landscape of that part of the Osage.

His life at the Blackjacks, about which I will have more to say in the next chapters, involved hunting, entertaining international guests, and smoking a pipe by a fireplace surrounded with bearskins and animals that Mathews himself had stuffed.[92] On the mantle was placed "the motto of [Mathews's] life at the Blackjacks," a Latin inscription Mathews had run across at a Roman officers' club excavation in North Africa: *Venari Lavari Ridare Occast Vivere* (To hunt, to bathe, to play, to laugh—that is to live).[93]

Although this life reflects Mathews's post-Oxford Anglophilia, anthropologist Garrick Bailey is certainly correct in saying that "his aristocratic bearing is possibly more typical of the Osage than of the English."[94] To historian Terry Wilson (Potawatomi), this lifestyle "conjure[s] a kind of Oklahoma Hemingway." Further, "the hunting jackets that he inevitably wore completed what might have been an irritatingly macho image had not his soft-voiced humor, respect for nature, and tribal education rendered him a wilderness sage, a gentler kind of Hemingway." After a decade of this single lifestyle Mathews married, but he remained at the Blackjacks until late in his life when poor health forced him back into Pawhuska.[95]

Near the time of his move to the Blackjacks, Mathews became an important figure in Osage politics. Elected to the tribal council in 1934, he served two four-year terms. During that period he was "the chief articulator of Osage wants and needs" and "always the first to speak when visiting dignitaries or technocrats from Washington were present," primarily because of his international experience and education rather than because of solid trust from other council members. His intimidating credentials caused some Osages to resent his prominence even as they recognized his value to them.[96]

Mathews's major political accomplishment during his tenure on the council was establishing the Osage Tribal Museum in 1938. The museum was the first of its kind and received the wholehearted support of Commissioner Collier.[97] Mathews gathered within it examples of Osage ceremonial and traditional cultural items, many of which had been put away as "bad things" with the advent of peyotism.[98] The museum would remain such a constant and personal concern of his until his death in 1979 that he was not beyond calling the staff at closing time to make sure the windows and doors were locked.[99]

Importantly, the passage of the IRA and the subsequent decline of concern for Native issues brought about a new situation for those who remained without a written intellectual voice. Many traditionalist Natives considered the IRA an illegitimate abrogation of treaty relationships with the United States and did not approve it. Other Native opponents of the IRA sought to reform the existing system, whereas some endorsed it and worked within its guidelines. When official suppression of traditional religion and politics ceased, many Native leaders who had been isolated for several decades began to come forward. Their impact continues to this day.[100]

Concomitantly, literary production by Natives declined rapidly and was done primarily by anthropologists or historians. The most well known is Ella Cara Deloria, the aunt of Vine Deloria Jr., whose posthumously published historical novel *Waterlily* and anthropological texts have become important in the recovery of Native intellectual traditions.[101] In this function her work is similar to that of Mourning Dove.

To understand the context of Mathews's work, then, is to understand a moment far different from that which produced the works of Eastman, Bonnin, Montezuma, and other SAI writers. The battle after World War II to end "termination," the 1950s federal policy that threatened to end all federal responsibility for American Indian groups, held little of the glamour of the integrationist project of the earlier period.[102] "Indians," according to Vine Deloria Jr., "had become an exotic and remote commodity fit only for perusal by tourists and those few people in Congress who had some local concern with them. World problems had now come to dominate the thinking of the American public."[103] Deloria says that the generation of organizational and tribal leaders that emerged during this period "formed a group that not only controlled much of Indian policy but also provided sage advice and acted as models for the younger generation. These people had read Felix S. Cohen's *Handbook of Federal Indian Law* by kerosene light in log cabins and were as competent in the niceties of legal fictions as most attorneys then representing the tribes."[104] Unlike the American Indians involved in national policy, Mathews and his writing contemporaries did little of the political associating with one another of the previous generation.

Mathews, because of his independent income, did not rely on the popularity of Indians in writing his books. Two of his works, the autobiography "Twenty Thousand Mornings" and his second novel, "Within Your Dream," remain unpublished. The books Mathews did publish have not had the impact of McNickle's, even though Mathews's work is, as I will argue in chapter 2, at least as sophisticated and critically interesting. *Talking to the Moon*, Mathews's philosophical reflection on ten years of living alone on the Osage prairie, draws little attention even from those few critics and historians who have written about Mathews. Another of his books is a biography of his friend and former Oklahoma governor and oil tycoon E. W. Marland. Mathews's final book, *The Osages: Children of the Middle Waters*, draws attention and admiration from those who write tribal histories, yet most academic historians are too perplexed by its lack of extensive footnotes to take it seriously.[105]

Mathews remained until his death in 1979 a cosmopolitan man whose sophistication and experience of the world far exceeded those of most of his readers in the isolated United States. Far from being intimidated by the U.S. Anglo intellectual figures in his day, Mathews found them too provincial for his liking. His disdain for the market and his relative economic privilege, unfortunately, obscured until recently his place in Native intellectual history. The same can be said for others whose works appeared between 1930 and 1960. Though beyond the scope of this present study, a refiguring of the period to take into account the multiplicity of voices has become an obvious necessity in American Indian critical studies.

This second moment of twentieth-century Native intellectual history did not so much dwindle as become replaced by another moment of Native intellectuals' coming together in a unified project. The time between the demise of SAI and the emergence of the National Indian Youth Council, however, remains important because of the growing respect for Native culture, variously envisioned, that the writers within it portrayed. Mathews, Ella Deloria, and McNickle—who helped directly to prepare the way for it—were the only figures of this second generation to see the emergence of the third period of American Indian intellectual history, when Native intellectuals undertook the project of making tradition the centerpiece of their political activism.

1960-1973: The Battle to Define "Red Power"

Three years after Mathews published *The Osages: Children of the Middle Waters*, a strange assortment of American Indians, journalists, political activists, white clergy, law-enforcement personnel, counterprotestors—and Marlon Brando—gathered on riverbanks in the state of Washington. On those rivers throughout 1964 and 1965, Natives from Northwest tribes asserted their treaty rights to fish in "usual and accustomed grounds," rights that the state did not recognize. Dozens of Natives were arrested for asserting these rights, and hundreds of Natives and their supporters from around the continent went to Washington to participate.[106]

Early on, the media were less than impressed. As Hunter S. Thompson reported for the *National Observer*, "The whole affair suffered badly from lack of organization. Mr. Brando was undoubtedly sincere in his effort; he talked persuasively and at great length about Indian problems, but he seemed to have no strategy except to get himself arrested."[107] What Thompson or anyone else could not have known was that by defying state law in full view of media and law-enforcement personnel, these Natives were among those initiating a new way of bringing their political struggles to the attention of the United States and the world. The series of events in Washington and other places continues to affect Native politics and intellectual discourse to the present day.

The fishing rights demonstrations were the first direct actions the National Indian Youth Council (NIYC), an organization founded in 1961 by young Natives disgruntled with the entrenched politics of their establishment elders, helped organize. D'Arcy McNickle and others in Indian affairs had much to do with the emergence of this group. As Deloria would later comment, the emergence of NIYC was yet another case in a long line going back at least to Pontiac and Tecumseh in which "what is certain in one generation is rigorously questioned in the next and the reverse holds also." At the same time he recognized that this particular generational conflict and questioning "opened up Indian affairs as it had never been opened, dividing the traditional government by consensus into a progressive movement with a majority and dissenting philosophy always opposing one another."[108]

This new, adversarial style and its attendant focus on press attention is seen first and perhaps best in the Pacific Northwest. NIYC president Mel Thom (Paiute) told Thompson:

> Long, too long, the State of Washington had been denying the Indians their treaty fishing rights and the Indians were never able to do much about it. Whenever the Indians got into federal court they won, but in local courts they never took the federal treaties laws into consideration. It looked hopeless. And the Bureau of Indian Affairs and the Department of Justice were very relaxed; they would not protect the Indians.
>
> Someone had to do something about it. And the Youth Council decided to go in with the Northwest Indians and stage the first tribal direct action in modern history.[109]

In gaining national attention for fishing rights in the Northwest and enlisting the support of national political organizations and celebrities, NIYC worked to achieve what no previous national Native organization had done: it tried to base its work in the day-to-day realities and political struggles of those reservation Natives who were the greatest victims of federal policy and local racism. With its ability to communicate with the U.S. government and the press, NIYC attempted to align itself with those who had been for a hundred years suffering in silence and neglect.[110]

Importantly, though, NIYC's founders were, like those of the Society of American Indians, largely educated professional Natives who were committed to working for their own people. Although Paul Chaat Smith (Comanche) perhaps chooses too strong a term in calling them "elitists," of crucial interest in understanding this period is that NIYC was made up of Native elites.[111]

After World War II, in which tens of thousands of American Indians had served in the U.S. Armed Forces, the U.S. government had created educational opportunities for this Native elite. The government expected these young people to become the Native leadership that would guide American Indian people into the mainstream of Euro-American values and society.[112] This was part of U.S. efforts starting in the early 1950s to terminate all federal services to American Indian groups, relocate Natives to metropolitan areas, and place responsibility for them in the hands of the states.[113]

This federal strategy was instrumental in creating a new generation for the Native political establishment that worked within the federal bureaucracy through the Bureau of Indian Affairs and the National Congress of American Indians, but many of the educated young people came to be radically critical of the mainstream and aggressively embraced their Native cultural traditions as both source and centerpiece of activism. They had seen returning veterans unable to find work and had grown up in the midst of poverty-stricken reservation communities. This led them to feel betrayed by a century of unkept promises from the paternalistic U.S. government, and, as Mel Thom said, "awareness of our situation . . . brought out anger. With anger and concern 'hope' was born. We were aware [that] if we did not take action, in our time, future generations of Indians would be denied the right to share our own heritage. . . . It was a matter of how to set up action to fight this threat."[114]

They came together at conferences and at summer workshops in Boulder, Colorado, that McNickle helped organize. Clyde Warrior (Ponca), one of NIYC's founders, became the most ardent spokesperson for and critical commentator on the increasing activity. "The unrest and resentment," he said, "has always existed through all the age groups of Indians. But the elders did not think anything could be done. Now they have young people coming home who are somewhat verbal, who have some knowledge of how the mechanics of government and American institutions work. It's a kind of happy meeting of elders . . . and these young people."[115]

Within this happy meeting, NIYC increasingly challenged the Native political establishment. Warrior called this group "Uncle Tomahawks," a sobriquet that, along with "apple'" (red on the outside, white on the inside), would be heard more and more often as the Indian world became politically polarized.[116] He published diatribes against the Bureau of Indian Affairs and these Uncle Tomahawks in NIYC's newspaper, *ABC: Americans before Columbus*. "I am disturbed to the point of screaming," he wrote in one editorial, "when I see American Indian youth accepting the horror of 'American conformity,' while those who do not join the great American mainstream of personalityless neurotics are regarded as 'incompetents and problems.' "[117]

Before his premature death in 1968, Warrior "came through Indian country like a storm," attempting to instill pride and raise consciousness among a people whose time, he believed, had come.[118] He believed that this new generation "must introduce into this sickroom of stench and anonymity some fresh air of new Indianness. . . . How about it? Let's raise some hell!" This fresh air, he wrote, "will not come about without nationalistic pride in one's self and one's kind."[119]

This generation of young intellectuals represents the beginning of the third important moment for twentieth-century Native intellectual history, another coming together into a common political project—finally ending the threat of termination and asserting through direct action the nationalism that had remained local for eighty years. The words of these figures reveal a central concern for critical reflection in the midst of political action. This reflection, as they practiced it, was not a domain belonging strictly to them. They sought a leadership style that would empower their constituencies to take control of their own lives. In the words of Clyde Warrior in 1967, "We must make decisions about our own destinies. We must be able to learn and profit from our own mistakes. Only then can we become competent and prosperous communities. . . . Too much of what passes for 'grassroots democracy' . . . is really a slick job of salesmanship."[120]

The newcomers were also concerned with presenting American Indians in their contemporary situation rather than in the pan-tribal vestments that had been popular among the SAI generation and would become the mainstay of the more militant leaders that would later emerge. They sought a nationalism that would draw its strength from the cultural, political, and religious traditions that the U.S. government had tried to stamp out, a nationalism that would at the same time adapt itself to the contemporary situation. "We have to fight in modern ways for the old ways," said Warrior. "Until we do that, it's all a lot of wishful thinking."[121]

This, then, was not the apocalyptic nationalism of the Ghost Dance movement nor was the only concern the day-to-day pragmatic need to bring money and programs to local communities. In confronting the issues of treaty rights and American Indian sovereignty, Warrior and the others battled on many fronts to create a nationalism that was both visionary and pragmatic.

Most important, they were committed to developing their nationalism on their own terms rather than uncritically importing ideas and strategies from other international movements. They owed much, of course, to decolonial struggles worldwide, African-American nationalism, and the Civil Rights movement insofar as they adapted slogans (Red Muslims, Red Power) and strategies from them. They carefully sought, however, to define their own ideology from the specific history and experiences of American Indian people.

The hell the young people raised, to use Warrior's phrase, was impressive. The fishing struggle received national attention and spawned other similar protests. The insurgents also put their establishment antagonists on the defensive with their diatribes and confrontational style in meetings.[122] This new focus on youthful energy was in large part responsible for Deloria's quick rise to power within American Indian politics.

Deloria was the executive director of the National Congress of American Indians (NCAI) from 1964 to 1967, when he entered law school at the University of Colorado.[123] His election to that position as a man in his early thirties reflects the growing trend toward younger Indian leadership even within the organization that had alienated its younger members only three years before. As he describes his elevation to the directorship, he had no official capacity at the 1964 annual convention and "wandered around . . . naively. The NCAI was undergoing one of its periodic purges and was looking for a new Executive Director. More of a pawn than an active candidate, I ended the week as the new director."[124] Like Mathews, then, Deloria learned the practical difficulties and complexities of federal Indian policy from the inside.

Along with his NIYC contemporaries, Deloria realized the need for thoughtful reflection in the midst of wholesale changes in Indian politics:

> You have to remember that everyone [Deloria and his contemporaries] came up during a time when it was necessary for Indians to fight like hell to be able to attend a conference on Indians, let alone speak. People find that hard to imagine today when the advice of every Indian is sought on every topic imaginable. Plus the older Indians were always scared that we would insult the powerful whites and they wouldn't help us any longer. So it was a time when everyone had to probe into what was possible and do whatever was needed. Imagine the 1961 Chicago conference where some hundred Indians gathered to put together a very poetic plea to JFK to treat Indians better and three years later, 1964, when it was popular for Indians to stand up and raise hell about being poor while a roomful of liberals wiped their eyes. Incredible changes happened and there were no good guidelines as to proper behavior.[125]

He further points out that although some of the antagonism between NCAI and NIYC was actual, much of it was created for publicity purposes.

Deloria was born in 1933 in Martin, South Dakota, a town that bordered the Pine Ridge Reservation. His Standing Rock Sioux and Episcopalian minister father, Vine Deloria Sr., "was an Indian missionary who served 18 chapels on the eastern half of" Pine Ridge.[126] "In those days," Deloria says of his childhood, "the reservation was isolated and unsettled. One could easily get lost in the wild back country as roads turned into cowpaths without so much as a backward glance."[127]

His most vivid memory, he says, was of visiting Wounded Knee and of having his father point out survivors of the 1890 massacre. That bloody day, he recalls, "was vividly etched in the minds of many of the older reservation people, but it was difficult to find anyone who wanted to talk about it."[128] The part of Pine Ridge that Deloria describes in these reminiscences is the Medicine Root District, in which the full-blood traditionals of the Oglala Lakota live. Many people there still converse normally in Lakota and are suspicious of the federal government and tribal councils created by the Indian Reorganization Act. Pine Ridge, like many reservations, is dominated at the level of federal politics by its agency town, Pine Ridge Village. The area to the north and east of the agency remains the locus of the most resistant and traditional Oglalas.[129]

From these roots in Martin and the eastern part of Pine Ridge, Deloria departed to attend prep school in Connecticut for the last two years of high school. In 1951 his family moved to Iowa from Martin. "I went back [to Martin] only once for an extended stay, in the summer of 1955, while on a furlough, and after that I visited only occasionally during summer vacations." During that period he attended the Kent School in Connecticut, was graduated from Iowa State University, served in the U.S. Marine Corps, and attended seminary at Augustana, later renamed the Lutheran School of Theology, in Chicago.[130]

In college Deloria's consciousness of the centrality of Native tradition to the Indian future grew.[131] It was in seminary also that he came to a critically antagonistic relationship with Euro-American Christian culture. He worked in a machine shop as a welder for the four years during which he attended Augustana and summed up his experience of theological education by saying, "In spite of its avowed goals of and tangible struggle with good intentions, [theological education] provided an incredible variety of food for thought but a glaring lack of solutions."[132] What was lacking in Western Christian theology, for Deloria, was a sense of how doctrines and creeds could possibly relate to the day-to-day struggles of human existence. "The solutions we find to pressing daily problems," he writes, "rarely come into the arena of creedal surety. The answers we find in the heat of battle and the quiet of meditation," on the other hand, "are answers to questions we did not think we asked."[133]

Though he remained involved in church politics, Deloria took a job after seminary in 1963 with the United Scholarship Service and administered a program that placed American Indian and Chicana/o young people in Eastern preparatory schools. As he says of the program, "I . . . was probably the only Indian my age who knew what an independent Eastern school was like. As the program developed, we soon had some 30 students placed." While working with the Scholarship Service, Deloria made a strong commitment to encouraging only students with adequate preparation to pursue education. "I didn't feel," he says, "we should cry our way into the schools; that sympathy would destroy the students we were trying to help."[134]

It was at this time that Deloria was elected executive director of NCAI and established himself as a major figure in national Native politics. Stan Steiner begins his 1968 reportage of these "new Indians" with a story of an after-dinner speech Deloria gave in the mid-sixties. Steiner quotes Deloria as saying that the Native way of life is superior to the mainstream (a comment he has repeated ever since) and, most important, asking questions that he continues to ask until the present: "What is the nature of life? It isn't what you eat, or whether you eat, or [whom] you vote for, or whether you vote, or not. What is the ultimate value of [human life]? That is the question."[135]

Committed to pragmatic politics and frustrated with the conference-centered approach of national Native politics, Deloria decided to attend law school at the University of Colorado. "It was apparent to me," he writes, "that the Indian revolution was well under way and that someone had better get a legal education so that we could have our own legal program for defense of Indian treaty rights." At the same time he began promoting the treaty-based activism of traditional people, such as those he remembered from his early days in the Medicine Root District of Pine Ridge. "The message of the traditionals is simple," he wrote in the *New York Times*. "They demand a return to basic Indian philosophy, establishment of ancient methods of government by open council instead of elected officials, a revival of Indian religions and replacement of white laws with Indian customs."[136]

As with so many of his contemporaries, what comes out of Deloria's writings is a portrait of a search, at once pragmatic and visionary, for answers to the problems of Native communities in the context of the world as a whole. Having experienced the educational system of mainstream culture and finding little of worth for the daily struggle for sane existence, he and others sought to affirm the values of Native traditions and hoped they could foster a moment in which Native communities could revive those traditions as part of the process of developing socially, economically, and spiritually.

With their embryonic neotraditional nationalism and commitment to grassroots adjustment to the contemporary reservation situation, these young public intellectuals had moved toward bridging a gap that the Society of American Indians had rarely seen or thought of crossing. But the revolution that the "new Indians" of the early and midsixties were preparing was the kind of revolution that would have met with more success had it happened at the time of SAI. The disarray of Native America by the 1960s had created a conflictual diversity in Indian communities that continues until this day.

The gap between the traditional nationalists and the mainstream-educated elite was only one of many gaps in need of a bridge by the late 1960s. The impressive achievements of Deloria's generation at the level of federal policy and national strategizing were overshadowed as the most disenfranchised Indian people on reservations and off began finding a strong and angry voice of protest. The speed with which new programs, new activist strategies, and new organizations appeared expanded Indian affairs, but, as Deloria commented, "The effect of this expansion was that programs quickly became filled with people who had little knowledge or experience of Indian communities. Young people were torn out of the student context and became national leaders overnight."[137] Thus, what was at its best a sincere and profound engagement in both visionary and pragmatic nationalism was largely overwhelmed by events that would come to dominate Indian affairs and redefine "Red Power."

By the late 1960s and early 1970s the diversity of viewpoints among North American Natives had become so pronounced that no group was able to unify all the various elements. Jack Forbes (Renape/Lenape/Powhatan) points out four categories of Natives during that period. First, he says, "are the 'traditionalist-nationalists.' These people feel that their nationality is Indian," and they do not participate in the colonial politics of the U.S. federal government. Second are the " 'secular nationalists.' These are predominantly urbanized Indians, who share the nationalism of the traditionalists but not the Native religion [in depth]. . . . They are potentially the most violent group." The third group is the "tribal pragmatists," who are "commonly . . . descendants of 'progressive' Indians from the nineteenth century. Many are Christians and belong to the economic elite of their reservation." The fourth group Forbes calls "Americans of Indian Descent," who have only nominal ties to traditional culture and "share the values of their white middle-class peers and oppose Indian nationalism."[138]

The most significant of these groups in the milieu of 1968 to 1973 were the secular nationalists, who fulfilled their potential for violence and militancy in various direct actions around the continent during that time. Unlike NIYC nationalists, who gave voice to their anger at conferences and in university classrooms, these urban nationalists were born into impoverished urban settings where anger is inbred. As part of the 1950s termination policy, the U.S. government had relocated many Natives from reservations in the hope that they would find employment and integrate into the mainstream, and by the mid-1960s nearly half of all U.S. Natives were living in urban areas.[139]

Though the term "urban Indian" has, following the days of movement militancy, come to represent only the militant Natives who emerged, generally, from the poorest ranks of Indians living in cities, Natives living in diaspora included people across a broad range of social and economic standings. Many, in fact, had arrived before the relocation program. Some succeeded as small business owners, others as professionals, still others as students and academics on urban campuses. Amid the upheaval of the African-American struggle for freedom, the campus-based free speech movement, antiwar radicalism, the second wave of feminism, gay liberation, flower children, Brown Power militancy, hippies, and yippies, those Indians living in the squalor and hopelessness of urban ghettos stood up and spoke with the loudest Native voice. They stepped through the widening cracks in U.S. society and sparked among Natives a new sense of aggressive action.

The differences between the diaspora and reservation movements were similar to those in African-American activism of the time.

Growing up on a reservation was in many ways parallel to the insulated life of African-American leaders who emerged from the segregated South, whereas the Native experience in the cities was like the situation that produced Malcolm X and other radical militant African-American leaders and activists.[140] The diaspora nationalists shared with their African-American and Chicana/o sisters and brothers a sense of complete alienation from the political processes that affected their lives, alienation that issued in threatened and actual violent confrontation with the U.S. political establishment.[141]

The first widely publicized action coming from the cities was the occupation of Alcatraz Island in 1969, which spawned similar takeovers around the continent. The action, with students from California colleges making up the majority of the initial occupiers, lasted for nineteen months. At about the same time a local group in Minneapolis calling itself the American Indian Movement (AIM) was organizing security patrols, modeled after the Black Panther Party and the Brown Berets, in Native neighborhoods and becoming a vocal opponent of federal programs that neglected the needs of Natives who lived in urban areas. Most people in AIM leadership were close in age to those in NIYC, but many of them had spent time in correctional institutions or on skid row rather than in university classrooms. By 1972 AIM was quickly becoming a national organization wielding considerable power with the media, white churches, and foundations.[142] Many other organizations, such as the American Indian Press Association and the ad hoc Convocation of American Indian Scholars, were also emerging at the time.

It was in the midst of these events that Deloria became a well-known writer. In 1969 he published *Custer Died for Your Sins*. He followed this up with *We Talk, You Listen* (1970), *Of Utmost Good Faith* (1971), a revised edition of Jenning Wise's *The Red Man in the New World Drama* (1971), *God Is Red* (1973), *The Indian Affair* (1974), *Behind the Trail of Broken Treaties* (1974), and *Indians of the Pacific Northwest* (1977).[143] In all of these works he continued his cohorts' earlier concern for critical reflection in the midst of political action and for developing political and cultural strategies that maintained Native culture while adjusting to contemporary challenges and necessities.

He attempted, further, to remind readers of the long history of Indian affairs and the generations of activists and tribal leaders who had worked to ensure the Indian future. This is most evident in *The Red Man in the New World Drama*. In the chapters he added to his edition of Jennings Wise's work, he traces the active involvement of these earlier generations and seeks to demonstrate that the watershed events that were occurring with such speed were best understood in the context of a much longer story. He says in his conclusion, "In every generation there will arise a Brant, a Pontiac, a Tecumseh, a Chief Joseph, a Joseph Garry, to carry the people yet one more decade further. The national Indian scene is conspicuous by the number of capable organizations that characterize it. Which group will ultimately prove to have built its future on important issues and which will have fallen by the wayside is yet to be determined."[144]

At the same time other publishing events, including Stan Steiner's *The New Indians* and Kiowa-Cherokee writer N. Scott Momaday's novel *House Made of Dawn* (1968) brought contemporary American Indian experience and political issues to widespread public attention for the first time since the reform movement of the 1930s.[145] Dee Brown's *Bury My Heart at Wounded Knee* (1970) provided a searing revisionist history of the American West that galvanized many people to American Indian issues.[146]

While these important political and publishing events were happening, the traditionalist movement on the reservations developed a strong grassroots constituency and responded positively to the radical nationalist sentiment of the diaspora movement. Because of "overtures" from traditional people, "many of the urban Indians began to show up on the reservations, seeking the tribal heritage which they had been denied. They became the most militant of the advocates of cultural renewal."[147] Unlike the earlier nationalist intellectuals, who returned to these same traditions equipped with education and exposure to national Indian politics, the dispossessed urbanites brought an ardent zeal and willingness to take extreme measures to achieve their goals.

This zeal and willingness was evident in the fall of 1972 during the Trail of Broken Treaties Caravan that resulted in the occupation of the Bureau of Indian Affairs headquarters in Washington, D.C.

The caravan included not only the diaspora radicals and reservation nationalists, but also people from NIYC, Native women's organizations, tribal governments, and several other organizations.[148] This coalition produced a document that called for a reopening of the treaty process and recognition by the Nixon administration of the coalition's nationalist goals.[149]

The caravan started in California and Washington State in October 1972 and held rallies and picked up supporters as it moved toward the District of Columbia, where it planned to present the "Twenty Points" document to federal officials during election week in November. Though the Nixon administration and various media portrayed the caravan as made up of urban radicals, it was in fact overwhelmingly comprised of reservation-based Natives.[150]

Upon arrival in the U.S. capital, the by-then nearly one thousand Native protestors discovered that their advance team had not made sleeping arrangements for them. They gathered in an auditorium of the BIA building and awaited word of where they would spend the night. Nervous Nixon administration officials had arranged for a large detail of law-enforcement personnel to be present, and the police began getting edgy as the Natives became more and more uneasy. Unable to control the crowd, the police began harassing some of the Natives and scuffles broke out. Soon the Natives organized themselves and forced the police out of the building.[151]

During the occupation AIM leaders Russell Means (Lakota) and Dennis Banks (Ojibwa) came to the forefront of the coalition, gaining national attention through their statements to the press and such actions as Means's use of a portrait of President Nixon as a shield.[152] Each time the occupiers feared an attempt by police to retake the building, they blocked doorways and windows with office furniture. This resulted in destruction of government property, but not to the extent that the press reported following the final settlement and subsequent departure of the protestors. Unfortunately, the occupation overshadowed the planned discussion of the Twenty Points document, and the caravan left the capital not having gained much except negative press attention and a cash settlement.

What became clear in Washington was that the nationalists would be unable to lure conservative Natives into their broad-based coalition. In Washington leaders of the National Tribal Chairman's

Association (created with the support of Vice President Spiro Agnew) and some career Native employees of the BIA rallied behind the Nixon administration to condemn the occupation. Although other elected tribal leaders and BIA Indian employees did support the nationalists, many used the situation as a means to broker better jobs within the bureau and to ensure the continuation of federal program money that Nixon had been funneling into conservative and moderate tribal councils.[153]

The Wounded Knee occupation occurred soon after the Trail of Broken Treaties Caravan and marks the conclusion of the political and intellectual moment that had begun over a decade before. The location is symbolically important, as that same spot eighty-two years before had also represented the end of a turning point in Native resistance.

At Wounded Knee the traditionals and urban nationalists once again joined together. Along with AIM leaders Means, Banks, Carter Camp (Ponca), and Clyde Bellecourte (Ojibwa), the occupation featured the strong presence of traditional spiritual leaders such as Leonard Crow Dog (Lakota) and Frank Fools Crow (Lakota). By the time of the occupation, many within AIM had committed themselves to making spirituality the central focus of the movement.[154]

For seventy-one days AIM and local Oglalas stayed within the hamlet, surrounded by the gathered forces of U.S. marshalls and various other law enforcement and military personnel. Ellsberg Air Force Base was on alert, and media from around the world came to observe. During the times of the most intense firefights, the night sky was filled with the trails of tracer bullets, and in open fields, eerily illuminated by flares, were heard the sounds of military communications. Young and elderly Oglalas who had intimate knowledge of the land regularly trekked back and forth across the perimeter to bring supplies and ammunition in.[155]

By the end of the occupation, Means and others had performed the Ghost Dance, two of the occupiers were killed by U.S. government bullets, and one member of the U.S. forces was paralyzed. Though they had not succeeded in their goal of securing Wounded Knee as a sovereign nation recognized by the U.S. government, "the Indians had developed," in Deloria's words, "a new pride in themselves which transcended tribal loyalties and instilled in Indian children everywhere the image of the brave Indian warrior, which had been missing from Indian society for two generations."[156]

The Trail of Broken Treaties Caravan and Wounded Knee were turning points for American Indian activism, and the changes they brought, positive, negative, and indifferent, continue to affect Native politics and intellectual praxis. Deloria's reaction to these events also represents a turning point in his own career and gives perhaps the best example of the various sides of the intellectual struggle and experience reflected in his writings. In one way, he retained the visionary pragmatism of his generation, hoping to make gains in an increasingly difficult situation. Before the BIA occupation, for instance, he called for a "common front" of Native organizations through which every segment of Native communities would have a voice.[157]

Though he expected any such unity to be tenuous and incomplete, he called for a division of political labor in which AIM would be the activist arm, NCAI would do lobbying, NIYC would organize youth, and the National Tribal Chairman's Association (NTCA) would handle the BIA.[158] The deep and abiding historical and political rift between the various components of Indian activism, however, precluded the sorts of alliances and coalitions that had been possible just a decade earlier.

The now entrenched lack of even provisional cohesion led to an increasing sense of cynicism in Deloria's mass-market publications, as well as the more obscure writings that reached a smaller non-Native audience. Though Indian activism came in this period to include those who had never before had voices, the media ascendancy of AIM and the treaty-based nationalists also brought with it the loss of critical reflection and adaptiveness that had characterized the earlier nationalism. The activists were able to get on TV, but to the public they mostly remained the romantic Indians of yesteryear and were not able to present to the United States and the world the fact of their contemporary existence.

Deloria watched the demise of the activist movement with a sense that important gains had been made but that fundamental problems of federal policy and public perception had not been addressed. Many legislative and political battles had been won, such as the final overturning of the termination policy (1972), the restoration of

Blue Lake to the Taos Pueblo (1970), the restoration of the termi-
nated Menominees (1973), and the final victory of the fishing-
rights cases in the Pacific Northwest (1973). At the same time Deloria commented that "policy-makers . . . have never really wanted
change." He felt "a sense of impending doom because of the long-
term nature of Indian problems with the federal bureaucracy."[159] In
other words, the various pieces of the Indian movement had won
many important skirmishes but had come little closer, really, to win-
ning the larger, long-term battle.

Though Deloria continued to support the activist movement in
books and in courtrooms, he recognized earlier than most people
that the energy for social change both in Indian country and in
mainstream, post-Vietnam America, had waned. He began working
pragmatically to fill the void of legal literature regarding treaty rights
so that future litigation would have a pro-Native theoretical stance
when cases reached courtrooms.[160] Various protests and direct actions occurred after the Trail of Broken Treaties and Wounded
Knee, but public and media sympathy for Native issues soon
reached an ebb, and the third important moment for Native intellectual history had come to an end.

1973 to the Present: Diversity, Party Lines, and the Need for Generational Perspective

As noted at the beginning of this chapter, one of the legacies of the
ferment of the 1960s and 1970s was the creation of American Indian studies programs in colleges and universities around the United
States. Many of the problems still remain that those programs were
addressing when Thornton made his comment in 1978 about Natives having no disciplinary traditions. The purpose of this chapter
has been to create a context from Native intellectual history for discussing how best to address those problems in later chapters.

Figures from this most recent period have similarities with each
of the previous three. Before pointing those out, I will briefly summarize the earlier periods. The post-Pratt generation, I have argued,
was marked by a strong sense of cohesion. This mainly economically

privileged group supported the progressive policies of the U.S. government and was considerably distanced from community constituencies. In their embrace of integrative and acculturative policies, they viewed themselves by and large as examples to reservation Natives of the necessity of cooperating with the U.S. government. As William Willard argues, they made themselves into surrogates for the colonizing United States.[161]

Following the decline of the Society of American Indians, the writers of John Joseph Mathews's generation did not come together in a cohesive way. Their smaller numbers and a general lack of attention in the United States to Indian affairs give their work great variety, from Mathews's highly localized work to McNickle's work on the national Indian affairs scene and from Mourning Dove's angry indictment of Progressive policy to Ella Deloria's liberal ethnographic work.

The third period, from the emergence of NIYC to the decline of AIM, saw first a rejection of elitism by a part of the Native elite well suited to deep critical and pragmatic reflection. The inability of organizations like NIYC and NCAI to create ferment at the local level among nonelites gave way to the emergence of the radical figures from the era of militancy. The watershed events from that period produced an explosion in the number of Indian voices that sought inclusion in questions of both day-to-day political realities and the shape of an Indian future.

As the activist movement was reaching its peak and declining in momentum, the gains initiated by the success of Deloria and Momaday and other figures in the late 1960s began to take hold. The writers who have emerged since are impressive not only for the fact that their number far exceeds the number of Native writers that had appeared in all other periods combined, but also because of the variety of genres they use and the diversity of perspectives from which they write.

After Momaday's *House Made of Dawn* won the Pulitzer Prize in 1969, major publishing houses made commitments to Indian authors and published many anthologies of short stories and poems by American Indians.[162] Following Momaday's example, the past twenty years have witnessed the emergence of several established Indian novelists, including James Welch (Blackfeet/Gros Ventre), Leslie Marmon Silko (Laguna), Gerald Vizenor (Ojibwa), and Louise Erdrich (Ojibwa).[163] Although these novelists have followed in Momaday's footsteps, they have not imitated his style. Along with these major figures many other Indians have written novels, so the contemporary scene includes a wide range of authors as well as styles.

A similar proliferation has occurred among American Indian poets.[164] This proliferation of work has also had the effect of making known to the public and to academia the fact that American Indian life and culture did not end in 1890 at Wounded Knee. American Indians have also entered disciplines in the humanities in greater numbers during these years. Unlike Mathews's generation, the decline of public political attention to Native issues in the midseventies has not slowed the steady flow of Native writing.

Of all of the periods, this most recent one is the most critically self-reflective and the most concerned with asking what American Indian intellectuals do. The most frequent theme of essays and articles on this topic has been a desire to find a way to unify the discourse.[165] Such calls for unity come most often from "hard-line" scholars who continue to draw inspiration from the activism of the 1970s.[166] This continued presence of hard-line voices and the emergence, for instance, of woman-centered and gay and lesbian voices are the most obvious intellectual legacy of the NIYC-AIM period. Contemporary Native discourse, though, also has important similarities with the two periods that preceded the 1960s.

In spite of the presence of American Indian studies programs, the past fifteen years, in fact, most resembles Mathews's nonunified generation. The much larger number of writers now than then tends to obscure this fact, as does a strong sense of loyalty among Native scholars. The differences among contemporary writers are at least as marked as the differences among those of Mathews's generation.

At the same time, much of the rhetoric and activity of the past twenty years has been about unifying these various pieces of the intellectual puzzle and finding cohesion-creating critical categories. Such unifying categories, however, obscure crucial differences in a discourse much in need of recognizing the variety of contemporary American Indian experiences. Cohesion, on this reading, is neither beneficial, possible, or necessary. Does not the story of SAI from the turn of the century, after all, demonstrate that unifying Native discourse ensures nothing beneficial to Indian people? And is it not possible to change the political commitment of Indian intellectual production and still emerge with a critical praxis as exclusionary as that of SAI.

Indeed, if nothing else, the analysis here highlights the generational nature of Native intellectual discourse. Much as Deloria has attempted to take into account those who have worked in Indian affairs before the watershed changes of the 1970s, I have sought here to make a case that writers going back at least as far as Samson Occom have grappled with many of the same issues that remain with us today. Finding in their work not only resources for self-determined Native engagement but also political commitments and intellectual praxes that are at times troubling is a double-edged sword that reminds us constantly of our own challenges and fallibilities.

Given this reading of American Indian writers of the past century, I have tried in the chapters that follow to keep in mind two observations. First, American Indian cultural and critical studies must be able to include a more inclusive range of issues and perspectives if it is to reflect the varied and often conflicting political, social, and cultural concerns of American Indian people and communities. This is especially important in addressing areas that remain, by and large, neglected in American Indian discourse, most notably economic and social class, gender, and sexual orientation.

Second, a maturing American Indian criticism must be self-consciously open-ended and prepared for the unexpected in order to take into account the plethora of genres and styles of historical, contemporary, and emerging American Indian writing and cultural expression. Without a framework that can make sense of science fiction as well as retold traditional tales, Native feminist theory as well as classical Indian oratory, and postmodern novels as well as as-told-to autobiographies, Native discourse risks bursting at the seams.

Because Deloria and Mathews work within just such open-ended frameworks and defy any parochial, essentializing interpretation, their writings provide an ideal way of addressing these issues.

2 / The Violation of Sovereign Land and Community in Deloria and Mathews

The intellectual historical mode of chapter 1 served to create a context for understanding the place of Mathews and Deloria among American Indian writers in terms of the impact of history on their works. In this chapter the focus shifts to the ways in which literature promotes a deeper insight into history. Mathews's *Sundown*, a novel about a complex moment of Osage history, complicates and problematizes many of the neat edges of the history presented in chapter 1. He enlivens that history through the voices of fictional characters. Here, then, we see the cross-fertilization possible between literature and history.

The way to that end is a demonstration of how reading across the texts of American Indian authors provides the best foundation from which to understand those works. Mathews, as I will argue, provides a vivid literary descriptive interpretation of American Indian contemporary existence. After reviewing that description, I will present how Mathews and Deloria understand the issues *Sundown* describes. The categories of land and community and their relationship to each other will become literary critical keys to unlocking the contours of the novel and the historical processes it describes, as we concern ourselves with a most basic literary critical question: how should we read *Sundown?*

Reading *Sundown*

In *Sundown*, John Windzer, the mixed-blood Osage father of Mathews's protagonist, gives his newborn son the name Challenge (Chal), saying, "He shall be a challenge to the disinheritors of his people."[1] The world into which Chal is born is the Osage Reservation in the 1890s. The challenge, in John Windzer's mind, was going to be primarily an economic and educational one. It turns out to be a religious one as well.

Mathews portrays John Windzer and other Osage mixed-bloods in the novel as optimistic about the Osage future. This optimism comes from the newly discovered oil resources under the reservation and the belief that the U.S. government would "do only what's fair" regarding development of that oil (8). The day after Chal's birth, John goes to the general store to buy cigars for the full-bloods and mixed-bloods who gather there each day. Oil and gas, as usual, are hot topics of their conversation. Importantly, though, talk does not turn toward politics or economics until the full-bloods have departed. These political realities—the tensions between Osage Progressives and sovereignty-minded full-bloods—surrounding the birth of Chal Windzer introduce us to the major themes of *Sundown*, themes that provide a frame for the issues of this chapter.

The story Mathews tells is not a happy one. In a way similar to the 1970s novel *The Death of Jim Loney*, by James Welch, *Sundown* chronicles the self-destructive descent of the mixed-blood protagonist into alcoholism, debilitating self-hate, and spiritual despair. Louis Owens (Creek), in fact, calls *Sundown* the introduction of "the modern American Indian novel" because it sets out a pattern that subsequent novelists follow.[2] Chal's decline, as Mathews presents it, begins with two simultaneous events when the protagonist is approximately seven years old. First, John Windzer decides to send Chal to a new private school rather than the U.S. government-run school to which other Osage parents are sending their children. Most critics have pointed to this decision and the process it begins as the crucial influence on Chal's self-hate and self-destruction. In doing so they highlight the conflict between traditional Osage life and assimilative Anglo education.

Only one of the critics, however, is primarily concerned with the political context in which that decision comes. This is unfortunate because, while John Windzer is preparing his son to go to the private school so that he can learn how to behave properly among civilized people (European-Americans), the U.S. government is betraying his and other progressives' optimism. This reading of *Sundown* attempts to integrate the obvious individual struggle of Chal with his own identity and the broader, communal political context in which Mathews places his characters.

The importance of the political context is clear early in the story when John Windzer realizes some of his ambition by becoming a member of the Osage Council. Soon after, in 1900, the commissioner of Indian affairs abrogated the authority of the council. Following this, an abject Windzer "became one who acted like a dog that had been whipped. His black eyes showed disillusionment" (59). Chal cannot help but notice this change in his father and has his first significant political thoughts. To him the U.S. government had "seemed always present" and "its presence had seemed always beneficent and protective" (60). This moment of political awakening is the context in which Chal goes to the private school. That decision is, of course, a battle for Chal's individual mind, but an important part of that battle is the undermining of Osage sovereignty and the repression of Osage traditional life of the period.

In spite of John Windzer's disappointment concerning the abrogation of the council, he continues to expose Chal to his European and Euro-American heroes, including William Jennings Bryan and Lord Byron (29, 50). He teaches Chal to work toward being worthy of citizenship in the United States and looks optimistically toward the time when Osages will become models of the capitalistic virtues of commerce and thrift (54). As in Osage society of the period in general, though, this optimism proves difficult to maintain.

Chal discovers these difficulties in school, at the state university, in the military, and when he returns to Osage County as an adult. In the private school he "associat[ed] himself almost entirely with the white boys" (68). During the years of his formal education, Chal experiences two feelings that will remain with him throughout the novel. First, he feels "ashamed" that on weekends he would go out alone, on horseback, to the prairies (68). Second, "He felt that there was something in him which must come out, and unable to find any other expression, he took action as a means, and raced his pony as wildly" as when he was a young boy (68-69).

When he rejoins his boyhood full-blood friends Running Elk and Sun-on-His-Wings in high school and they ride out to the prairie together, "He felt that some kind of glory had descended upon him, accompanied by a sort of sweetness and a thrilling appreciation of himself. He wanted to struggle with something" (73). True to his father's influence, though, Chal suppresses the feeling and finds himself "deliciously unhappy" (73). He experiences psychologically what Pratt's students at Carlisle experienced physically—the denial of the value of traditional customs and culture in favor of the "civilized" values of the dominating society.

The split between these values becomes most extreme when Chal, Running Elk, and Sun-on-His-Wings go to university together. All three become members of the football team and of the same fraternity. On the train that takes them to the university, Chal looks out the window and observes the many ugly towns built by whites after the Oklahoma land rushes of the late nineteenth century. He does not vocalize his disgust. Rather, "He kept this feeling subdued; kept it from bubbling up into the placid waters of his consciousness, so that nothing would disturb those waters to keep them from reflecting the impression that ought to be mirrored, if one were to remain in step" with proper Euro-American values (90).

The two full-bloods are also silent, but not out of a desire to impress the Anglos. Their expressionless faces hide their deep suspicion and resentment toward the contradictory white values they have decided to endure in order to play football. The breaking point for these characters arrives at the time of their fraternity initiation. One of the fraternity men calls on the three Osages to come forward to be paddled. Chal steps forward and allows the white fraternity man to humiliate him. Sun-on-His-Wings and Running Elk, however, refuse to submit and the next day pack their bags in disgust and leave the university (106-13). Chal "felt a little angry with them, and with all the others at home because they were so backward about taking up civilized ways of talking and acting. He knew he was going to stick it out" (112).[3]

Chal does stick it out but finds himself unable even to carry on conversations because he is so worried that he will reveal himself to be uncivilized. He develops an infatuation for a white sorority woman, Blo Daubeny, but cannot speak to or entertain her when they go out on dates. After one particularly unsuccessful evening with her, Chal declares to himself, "I wish I didn't have a drop of God damn Indian blood in my veins" (160). Unhappy with school, and with World War I under way, he decides to join the military.

These self-hating statements and sentiments continue in the military. During his time in the service he has an affair with an Anglo woman, assuaging her fear of his dark skin by telling her that he is Spanish (203). The action of flying an airplane gives him the most satisfaction of his life, and "he thought of himself as being separated by a great abyss from Sun-on-His-Wings and Running Elk, and from the village with the people moving among the lodges" (208). The respite from confusion, though, is short-lived. Chal has to return to the Osage after his father is killed by white bandits in search of Osage money, and Chal once again feels the unhappiness that has plagued him from the time he was a young boy (235, 245).

Chal inherits his father's small fortune but is not able to find a business venture in which to invest. The rest of the novel chronicles his slow decline into alcoholism.[4] He does little but ride around in his big car, get involved with gold-digging women, and drink bootleg whiskey in dance halls and at all-night parties. The events of these last chapters are a combination of drunkenness and religious experience.

He takes two young white women to the summer ceremonial dances. The women encourage him to take them because they want to have an exotic experience of real Indians doing Indian things (252). Yet, once at the dance arbor, Chal is not ready to leave when the women grow tired of observing the friendly natives. As he watches, he recalls his childhood and his dancing and singing on the prairies of older days. The sound of the drum pulls him into memory and he considers dancing the next year (264).

In the next chapter, after a long, all-night party, Chal finds himself in a ceremony with his friend Sun-on-His-Wings, who has become a peyotist. The worshipers, Mathews writes, "were influenced very slightly by that which they called the Great Frenzy [and] lived their daily lives as the fathers had lived, dressing in their leggings, blankets, and bandeau" (266). While in the lodge, Chal drinks some of the hallucinogen and has to go outside to vomit. Sun-on-His-Wings joins him and says, "That is the evil that has come out of your body" (269).

Back inside, Chal settles into a dreamlike state that is interrupted only when one of the worshipers asks the leader, called the Road Man, a question about how to deal with the murder of his son. The Road Man makes a long speech, a section of which is worth quoting at length:

> Long time ago there was one road and People [Osages] could follow that road. They said, "There is only one road. We can see this road. There are no other roads." Now it seems that road is gone, and white man has brought many roads. But that road is still there. That road is still there, but there are many other roads too. There is white man's road, and there is road that comes off from forks. The bad road which no white man follows—the road which many of the People follow thinking it is the white man's road. People who follow this road say they are as the white man, but this is not white man's road. People who follow this road say that road of Indian is bad now. . . .
>
> The road of our People is dim now like buffalo trail across prairie. We cannot follow this road with our feet now, but we can see this road with our eyes, and our hearts will go along this road forever. Even if our bodies are carried by our feet on this road that is not Indian road. There are few of us whose eyes can see old road of our People, I believe. (271)

After the ceremony Chal feels "a keenness that he had not felt for days; an exhilaration that made everything interesting" (277). Chal is able to see in the experience of the peyotists his own experience and is tempted to join them in their religious way of life, but he soon resists the impulse.

In the next and penultimate chapter, Chal finds himself at another all-night party. He departs the party, buys some bootleg whiskey, and speeds around the dirt roads of the county in his roadster. He is thrilled by the speed of the car but stops and gets out because he "felt he had to express himself in some bodily action" (296). The section that follows captures a major theme of *Sundown*:

Suddenly, he began to dance. He bent low over the grass and danced, and as he danced he sang, and as he sang one of the tribal songs of his people, he was fascinated by his own voice, which seemed clear and sonorous on the still air. He danced wildly and his blood became hotter, and yet that terrific emotion which was dammed up in his body would not come out; that emotion which was dammed up and could not be expressed. As he danced he wondered why that emotion which had begun to choke him did not come out through his throat. He was an Indian now and he believed that the exit of all spirit and emotion was the throat, just as the soul came out through the throat after death.

He was in pain and he danced frantically for some sort of climax; that sense of completeness that consummates the creative urge; an orgasm of the spirit. But he couldn't dance fast enough, and his singing lacked the fire to release his dammed up emotion.

The dance became wilder and suddenly, in his despair, he broke the rhythm of his singing and yelled, but still his emotion was choked in his body. He wanted to challenge something; to strut before an enemy. He wanted by some action or some expression, to express the whole meaning of life; to declare to the silent world about him that he was a glorious male; to express to the silent forms of the blackjacks that he was a brother to the wind, the lightning and the forces that came out of the earth. (296-97)

A few lines later, after the dance has exhausted him, Chal looks at the blackjacks, the running scrub oaks that grow throughout the area, and wonders about their "perfect patience . . . on still days; perennially waiting for something" (297). He finishes the rest of his whiskey and falls asleep on the ground.

Chal's mother begins emerging from the shadows of the story as *Sundown* moves toward its conclusion. In the earlier sections of the novel she had kept her thoughts to herself and allowed John Windzer to guide Chal's life. Mathews never even gives the woman a name. Her unspoken frustrations with her husband's decisions provide the second important influence on Chal throughout the novel.

Unlike the great majority of novels featuring American Indian mixed-blood protagonists, both of Chal's parents are Natives. His mother comes from an Osage full-blood family. In spite of her formal importance to the story, Mathews's portrayal of her is part of his consistently baffling treatment of women. For example, Mathews has Chal's mother refer to John Windzer as her "lord" (23, 57). Such language is odd. During the economic boom period that Mathews describes in *Sundown*, "All Osage women were . . . economically liberated from any forced dependence on male financial support." Though they would not be enfranchised in Osage political structures until 1944, Osage women carried considerable social and political clout throughout the period.[5]

The unnamed mother takes on importance in the midst of Chal's intense struggle with himself. At the same time, the U.S. government finally begins looking into the various murders and swindles that have occurred during the Great Frenzy. In the final chapter Chal attends the hearings and is at first alarmed and embarrassed when a full-blood, Roan Horse, stands up to address the investigators and insists on doing so in the manner of a traditional orator. He settles himself into position as if he were going to proceed on a long oration. However, he says simply, "Gentlemen of the senatorial investigating committee: I am Roan Horse. I say this to you. You have come here twenty-five years too late" and sits down (306).

The crowd laughs at the way this proud, dignified, unbent Osage is able to make fools of those who were pretending to care about what their government had been sponsoring for a generation. Where were they, Roan Horse is asking, when this process of disinheritance and oppression was beginning? Why had they come to investigate only after so many Osages had died or had lost their money and after the group was so demoralized that its integrity as a people was undermined? "Chal," Mathews writes, "felt quite proud of him" (306). This is the turning point in Chal's perceptions of the experiences through which he and other Osages had lived.

Chal understands, finally, that the Progressive economics and politics of his father and the mixed-bloods have only fueled the desires of whites to separate Osages from their wealth. Because of the Great Depression, however, "the representatives of civilization changed from jovial backslapping, efficient people, around whom he had placed an aura of glory, to dour, reticent people who seemed afraid" (307). This critical stance toward the Progressives, importantly, does not lead him to embrace the full-bloods totally. Even though they are vindicated vis-à-vis the mixed-bloods, "Chal was annoyed that they didn't seem to be aware that something important had happened to the little world of their blackjacks and prairie" (308).

In the last pages of the novel Chal has a conversation with his unnamed mother about his future. She had always hoped he would be a warrior and, with classic traditional indirection, suggests that Chal go back into the military. "An intense urge flooded him," Mathews writes of Chal, "an urge to vindicate himself before this woman. . . . Then suddenly he was warmed by a thought. There was a primordial thing which thrilled him and made his stomach tingle, and he felt kindly toward his mother—toward this Indian woman who could see into a warrior's heart" (310).

Chal tells his mother that going back into flying will not be his path, but that he had recently thought about going to law school. Both Chal and his mother recognize in him something they had not seen for years. Chal, Mathews says, "experienced an assurance and courage that he hadn't felt for years," and his mother "saw a little boy in breech clout and moccasins holding up a cock sparrow for her approval" (311). The novel ends without a hint of whether or not Chal goes to law school.

Sundown, as the second of Mathews's five books, written on the tails of the success of *Wah'Kon-Tah,* is a book Mathews did not seem to care much about. He told Charles Larson in a letter:

> After the success of *Wah'Kon-Tah* I was asked to go to New York and once there the publishers hounded me to write a novel and somehow in the confusion I did promise to write one.
>
> I am a hunter by nature and once home in the Blackjacks the Quail season was open and I found myself wanting to hunt instead of wanting to write. I finally sat down to write the book without any inspiration. Sent it off to the publisher where it was accepted readily.[6]

If Mathews could have known in advance some of the ways his only published novel has been interpreted, he would perhaps have saved the postage and used the pages of the manuscript to wrap his season's take of quail.

Larson's evaluation of the novel is by far the weakest. He says, "By the end of the story, [Chal] is utterly passive, plagued by guilt because of his feelings about his racial identity." He calls Mathews an "assimilationist" who believed that "the horrors of the recent past . . . had apparently shown . . . the total destruction of tribal life and the need for acceptance of the white man's way of life" and that Mathews reveals only a limited concern with the social issues confronting Native Americans of the time."[7] Larson thus reduces *Sundown* to the individual identity struggle of Chal and completely ignores the fact that the story parallels exactly the social issues confronting Osages of the period.

Andrew Wiget finds in *Sundown* only a "partial artistic success" of "tiresome pace" about a character "caught between two worlds." Chal's decline into alcoholism represents a "character all too familiar" in American Indian fiction, "paralyzed . . . alienated . . . and inarticulate."[8] He takes exception to Larson's comments but still emphasizes Chal's identity struggle as strictly biological-cultural rather than political-ideological. Quite obviously, though, Mathews did not intend *Sundown* to be merely a story of how an individual deals with personal identity. Rather, Mathews evokes a historical period of intense importance for Osage people and communities and attempts to sort out how the political strategies of various groups of Osages played out and what possible future might exist.

On that reading Mathews creates a framework in *Sundown* through which he shows how the Osage Progressives were overoptimistic in believing that the U.S. government would deal with them justly and that they could assimilate Anglo values and be accepted as full citizens. However, he does not uncritically endorse the full-blood faction in their noncooperative stance. Chal remains worried to the end that they do not know that something has changed and that they will also have to change. *Sundown* is not, as Wiget's and Larson's analyses would have it, a story of the conflict between white and Indian values, but a nuanced description of what Mathews saw as the weaknesses of two internal political and social strategies in the midst of an oppressive situation.

Carol Hunter, a mixed-blood Osage, traces many of these historical themes in two essays about the novel.[9] In one, she carefully sets out the historical figures and events Mathews alludes to in the novel and demonstrates without a doubt that the novel cannot be reduced to a simple story of an individual's identity struggle. She argues, "It is from the historical context that the novel's message emerges." In both essays, Hunter places the novel in its political and historical context and points out that Mathews did not want to tell the story of just one person, but of a community in religious, political, and economic crisis. She concludes that Mathews wrote the novel to show "Challenge's generation as tragic victims of abrupt assimilation."[10]

Owens's recent study is the most careful and astute to date. With sharp sight he analyzes the various elements of the story and argues that Mathews's story is one of "rejecting the cliché of the Vanishing American as epic, tragic hero." Owens reads the novel as a "repudiation of the simple, entropic plot assigned to the American Indian by Euramerican myth-making."[11] I wish to take Owens's comments one step further by asking how Hunter's language of tragedy, victimization, and alienation, in spite of her keen historical insights, is a barrier to uncovering what Mathews perceived was happening to Chal Windzer and his generation.

The suggestion here is not that such categories necessarily do not work for American Indian literature. Hunter's categories, in fact, accurately describe the work of Mathews's contemporary D'Arcy McNickle in his novel *The Surrounded*. In that work, a protagonist with a Spanish father and a Native mother returns to his reservation home and, through a series of events, is accused of two murders that he did not commit. He is a powerless figure whose destiny is foreordained.

Larson calls McNickle "the earliest Native American prose stylist, the earliest craftsman of the novel form" and counts him among the more accomplished writers of the 1960s and 1970s rather than among Mathews and his other contemporaries. For Wiget, *The Surrounded* "surpasses . . . artistically" Mathews's novel. McNickle's "grimly deterministic story" once again is given a much more sympathetic reading than *Sundown*.[12]

This strong praise for McNickle and ambivalence toward Mathews raises some important points. Both critics project the former as telling a more nuanced and epic story. Such evaluation, however, is difficult to justify. Mathews, through a protagonist who is the child of a full-blood mother and mixed-blood father, tells a story of a community in crisis. The conflicts within that crisis follow with exacting detail actual events of Osage communities of the period. Chal's struggle with identity becomes a lens through which to understand a struggle of immense and confusing proportions.

McNickle, at least in the published version of his first novel, tells the much less complex story of a child of Native and Anglo parentage struggling with individual identity.[13] The surrounded world the novel exposes is that, in the main, of one family. The lens *The Surrounded* provides is one of a general metaphysical struggle between Indians and whites with one person stuck in the middle.

This harsh evaluation of *The Surrounded* is aimed more at critics than at McNickle, whose crucial literary and political contributions to American Indian life are highly deserving of attention. The fondness with which many people who encountered him at the Boulder workshops or in local communities remember him is further evidence of his important contribution to Native life. But *The Surrounded* preceded McNickle's career in Indian affairs. Thus it is best understood in the context of his New York period, when his major concern was for his own writing career rather than for Indian communities (or identity).[14] It is telling that this novel, which, compared to *Sundown*, Mourning Dove's *Cogewea*, or even McNickle's later work least reflects American Indian community life, is the one most often singled out for critical attention. And when critics have attended to *Sundown*, most often they have approached it with the same expectations as McNickle. My argument is that Mathews's novel and his other works are attempts to challenge the language of victimization, tragedy, and alienation that Hunter applies to him and that McNickle uses.

We turn now to another way of reading the story told in *Sundown*. Of crucial importance to that alternative is Mathews's *Talking to the Moon* and a discussion of how that work provides a way of understanding the biological, social, and religious backdrop against which Chal's generation lived. Following this, an analysis of Deloria's similar, though significantly different, approach to these same issues will be instructive.

The first priority of developing American Indian criticism is to step back from current critical strategies and find within the internal variety of historical and contemporary voices the sources of such a criticism. A critical accounting of the differences between Deloria and Mathews illustrates what such an approach can produce and what sorts of resources are available.

The key to understanding how Mathews and Deloria, in the midst of their differences, both come to a critical understanding of the most crucial challenges of American Indian people comes from their thoughts on land and community. On the subject of land Mathews provides a depth of analysis that tends to complete what is only sketched in broad strokes in Deloria's work. In the area of community, Deloria's more direct analysis offers a way of opening up obscurities in Mathews.

From this review emerges an understanding of the challenges facing American Indian communities in the twentieth century. Both John Joseph Mathews and Vine Deloria Jr. locate those challenges in the different cultural, political, and religious viewpoints on community, land, and sovereignty held by Native communities and in the dominating material culture of the United States. Though their approaches are different, each writer provides a thoroughgoing critique of that dominating culture. This critique functions as the foundation for their analyses of contemporary American Indian internal situations.

Talking to the Moon When No One Listens

John Joseph Mathews says that when he returned to Osage County in 1929 he "wasn't running from anything." Whatever the truth of that statement, both he and the county were different from what they had been when he had left only a few years earlier.[15] Mathews had received a degree in natural sciences from Oxford, had lived in Switzerland and Los Angeles, had traveled throughout Europe and North Africa, and had married and divorced. As for Osage County and the people living there, Osage traditional life and the landscape

itself had changed considerably. Many animal species had disap-
peared, and the complex social and ceremonial system in place just
forty years before was all but completely supplanted.

In spite of these changes, some parts of the culture and the landscape remained similar to prereservation days. Some people did not
join the peyotists or Christian churches and maintained remnants of
the older ways, and coyotes, deer, bobcats, wild turkeys, and other
animals still roamed freely through much of the county.[16] The
blackjacks also remained, except where they had been trampled by
the large herds of cattle or destroyed by oil development.

Talking to the Moon, the book of observations gleaned from the
ten years Mathews lived alone on this changed and changing landscape, is deceptively subtle. At first glance it might seem a simple
telling of interesting anecdotes, along with a few sections of social
commentary about World War II. Its subtlety, perhaps, explains the
neglect it has suffered among those who read American Indian literature.[17]

The book is organized into fourteen chapters, the first two describing the building of Mathews's house and the reasons for his return to the Osage. The next twelve chapters are divided into four
sections, representing the four seasons of three months each. He des-
ignates each chapter with the descriptive name Osages traditionally
give to the cycles of the moon, the first being "Just-Doing-That
Moon," roughly March or the beginning of springtime, the last in
the cycle being "Light-of-Day-Returns Moon," roughly February or
the last days of wintertime.

More than simple nature writing, *Talking to the Moon* is an interpretation of the ecological and social history of the Osage land and
people. It is imbued throughout with a largely accurate, tragic sense
that in only a few years most of these things, too, except the blackjacks, will pass into memory. Less than a half-century after its writing, many of the animals that were common in Mathews's time are
rare or nonexistent sights. Now, rather than the eldest Osages being
able to remember the last buffalo hunts, the move to the reservation,
and the ceremonial system, the eldest are the last to remember those
who remembered these things.

When he moved into his sandstone house, named the Blackjacks,
on the prairie in 1932, Mathews says he was seeking "to devote a

few years to pleasant and undisturbed living" (3). The decade he ended up living in that house followed the Great Frenzy of Osage oil exploration. Mathews's years on the Osage Tribal Council and the implementation of Roosevelt's Indian New Deal also occurred during this period. These years witnessed tremendous upheaval and ferment in the United States and around the world: the Great Depression and the co-optation of radical politics in the United States, the rise of German Nazism, World War II, the ascendancy of Stalinism in the Soviet Union, the full-fledged anticolonial rumblings of the European colonies, and the ferment surrounding the Harlem Renaissance are just some of the world events that were going on as Mathews removed himself from "the roaring stream of civilization" (11).

As for the land on which he lived, oil wells had cluttered once-open vistas, and the periodic and easily predictable droughts of the Plains had stripped significant amounts of irreplaceable topsoil from the lands that Osages and other American Indian groups had ceded to the U.S. government in the previous century. This was at least the third time in that period that drought had stripped the land, aided by unsuitable agricultural practices and ideologically motivated land speculation. The resulting dust bowl displaced white, African-American, and American Indian farmers who had plowed up much more land than they could cultivate given the demands of the Plains climate. After less than a century of Euro-American domination, the land was bereft of millions of buffalo and other animals and could no longer bear, without chemicals and modern machinery, the agricultural system that had replaced these animals.[18]

This "disaster," as Mathews calls it, "was the natural result of [human] shortsightedness in ravaging the land" (16). That same lack of foresight, he argues, caused many of his contemporaries not "to realize they were experiencing the end of an era," an era of "flush production" in which a group "had eaten the frosting from the cake and had never been taught that the layers underneath were edible" (15, 16). Like the Progressives in *Sundown*, Mathews's contemporaries could not yet imagine that the optimistic excesses of the 1920s would not continue.

Mathews had little pity for these shortsighted people and groups. Rather, he saw them as paying the price for their own arrogance.

Though he had once worshiped "the crowding and elbowing of [people] in Europe and America . . . [and the] clanging steel and the strident sounds of civilization," he had realized that "by the realization of such dreams [people] had begun thinking they were cutting their bonds with the earth; that they had torn themselves loose from the restrictive laws of biology" (2, 3).

Although he drew these "laws of biology" from his formal training at the University of Oklahoma and Oxford, Mathews's articulation of how these laws work in his environment and among social groups is not a doctrinaire pronouncement. He bases his thoughts on what he could observe going on around him. Also, he obviously gained much from his friendship with, among others, Paul Sears, the scientist who first described ecology as "the subversive science."[19] To understand Mathews it is necessary to resist isolating his theories and subjecting them to scientific analysis; instead, one must comprehend something of the life he led at the Blackjacks.

Though in many ways a lonely existence, that life saw a steady flow of visitors. Sears, an advocate of Frederic E. Clements's still-influential climax theory of ecology, was one of the many international friends of Mathews who visited the Blackjacks, usually in July (97).[20] As Mathews describes them, these visits from friends centered on food, conversation, and journeys onto the prairie. "If there is no venison or bear left over from my last hunt in my cold-storage locker," he writes, "there are great cuts of choice beef to be served with spaghetti, or I fry a chicken for each person present, or roast a guinea or pheasant for each person, but always have spaghetti" (98). Thus, as Sears, among others, obviously influences Mathews in *Talking to the Moon*, that influence does not come in the way a university student learns from a professor, but as a friend whose influence results from long walks on the blackjack ridges and from ideas and theories shared over dinner and into the late night.

In Mathews's life at the Blackjacks we find an extreme precursor to N. Scott Momaday's admonition, three decades later:

> Once in [their] live[s people] ought to concentrate their mind[s] upon the remembered earth, I believe. [They] ought to give [themselves] to a particular landscape in [their] experience, to look at it from as many angles as [they] can, to wonder

about, to dwell upon it. [They] ought to imagine that [they]
touch it with [their] hands at every season and listen to the
sounds that are made upon it. [They] ought to imagine the
creatures that are there and the faintest motions in the wind.
[They] ought to recollect the glare of noon and all the colors of
the dawn and dusk.[21]

What Mathews developed and confirmed through just such observation and conversation were the two sets of biological laws he describes in *Talking to the Moon*. The first set is discussed in the beginning of the book and is, in one way, quite simple.

Biology, Mathews believed, is interested in all species as repro-
ducers and protectors of their offspring (12). These two laws, reproduction and survival, are for Mathews "primal" (12). More compli-
cated was Mathews's belief in the biological urge he observed in all
species for "ornamentation"—"useless" (as in utility) in the case of
all life-forms, "artificial" in the case of those humans who had invented the ornaments of "civilization" he had grown to abhor (12).
This urge for ornamentation, as far as Mathews was concerned, provides the key to understanding the situation modern humans find
themselves in:

> Deep in my consciousness was the conflict between [humans']
> dreams which create the magic of [their] civilization as well as
> [their] fumbling toward God; the dreams which create [their]
> ideologies and create beauty; the conflict between these
> dreams and [their] slavery to the primal laws of survival and
> reproduction. (16)

By thinking themselves divorced from these processes, Mathews believed, humans were expressing an arrogance that was understand-
able but profoundly sad because of its irreversible effect upon the
land and the peoples who had lived there for thousands of years.

The indigenous Osage inhabitants, before the arrival of Euro-
Americans, had lived with the same ornamental urge but had expressed it in a fashion that was in accord with the primal laws:

> Their religion, their concept of God, came out of my black-
> jacks, out of the fear inspired by the elements, and it was col-
> ored just as the animals were colored for perfect adjustment.
> Of course, it was the result of [human] imagination and [their]

dreams and fears. Even though primitive [people] had the distinction among the animals of being able to think, [they] were not by reason of their mental powers the "insurgent[s]" which some anthropologists choose to call [them]. [Their] mental processes were still under the influence of the natural background, and the Osage religion of Wah-Kon-Tah was as much a product of the blackjacks and the prairie as the physical [human]. (77-78)

Mathews's "of course" in this quotation conceals the importance of this statement. Though he uses the word "primitive" to describe Osages before the arrival of the Europeans, he is not removing from them the same biological urges and motivations as other humans. Further, he makes the land itself an agent in the process. Elsewhere in the book he states, "I felt that even the backdrop and the stage were actors in our little drama, and the sense of intimacy grew with the finding of the evidence of that which had been academic knowledge" (29).

Mathews does not describe the other set of biological laws until the penultimate chapter of the book, though it, more than the "primal" laws of reproduction and survival, provides the foundation for understanding this and his other works. In his observation of life on the prairie, he came to believe that human societies, as outgrowths of the same life force as the rest of the world, developed in four stages. The first stage is that of youth and survival, of which play is a part. Mathews sees in the play of animals preparation for survival on the ridges around his house. Thus, dogs and coyotes romp with their siblings, learning how to fight while keeping their vulnerable front legs out of the way of another animal's fangs. Play is also a part of life for older animals, as a means of remaining constantly prepared and for wooing reproductive partners. But play is most important in the first stage of life because of the role it plays in later survival (215-17).

The second stage Mathews calls "virility." This and the other stages, which occur after life-forms have learned *how* to survive, depend on the observation Mathews makes about the ample, though limited, amount of life force that exists in nature:

Nature utilizes every square inch of my blackjacks for the existence of the species, and every spark of the life-force is utilized. When the forms in the stage of senility no longer are able to use the life-force which they acquired in their virility and utilized in their maturity, this life-force must be utilized by virility in its growth to climax. This must apply to [humans], since [they are] of the earth. (229)

Virility is the stage at which life-forms are finding their place in an environment. Maturity follows virility, when a life-form has established itself and has created a system by which its day-to-day survival is not as much in question. Survival for a mature form depends not on its ability to fight for space, but rather on its strength in fending off virile forms that try to acquire its space.

When the mature form begins losing this battle, the final stage, which Mathews calls senility, is setting in. This is the stage the virile forms wait for, when they can exploit the decline of the mature species. "The species of my ridges that do not attain their climaxes [maturity] remain intensely virile and await the inevitable decline of the senile, no matter how long they must wait, and virility remains always a 'danger' to senility" (230).

Mathews, unfortunately, uses the gendered term "virility" throughout most of the book. Only in a secondary way does he relate these biological terms to the separation, traditionally, of Osages into two major groups. Osages, as he recounts it, call these groupings Chesho [Tzi-Sho] for the Sky People and Hunkah for the Earth People" (221). These terms describe basically the same process as virility and maturity, but without the sexist implications.

With this interpretive scheme, Mathews declared that he was not so concerned with academic evaluation as he was with watching the theory work itself out in the life around him. "I was thwarted," Mathews says of writing the book, "by my own informality and defeated through my own inability to reason with those who had formal training. I could not begin with the upper branches of a tree and follow one to the trunk, but must go to the roots, and beyond the roots to the reasons for nature's encouragement of the seedling" (3). Evaluating these two sets of biological laws according to the principles of environmental science, sociology, or anthropology is thus not of primary importance, even though many of the ideas Mathews expresses are in accord with much of what contemporary theorists posit in these areas.

His statement about roots and branches, as the remainder of the book shows, is not mere metaphor drawn from nature, but is the actual way Mathews works to understand the world in which he lived. These theories of primal laws and natural progression do not provide predictive foundational surety from which Mathews draws a reductionistic analysis of how humans ought to *imitate* the rest of nature. He recognizes, in fact, the great variety of how different living things express the movement through the stages he identifies, and he does not find in the behavior of nonhumans a map for human societal behavior. Further, his is not a strict "natural law" scheme in which actions are circumscribed, but a framework in which biology determines and limits the options of human (as well as other species') agency. The purpose of observation and interpretation is to "return to the earth to ascertain where [humans have] diverged from the natural processes" (226).

This is the historical and geographical context in which Mathews returned to the Osage and developed his organic methodological perspective. More than looking for escape, he returned with many questions that his cosmopolitan experience had raised but not answered:

> I came to the blackjacks as a man who had pulled himself out of the roaring river of civilization to rest for a while; out of the flood where formerly only his head had been above the surface. Stopping for a time and looking back, he could better appreciate the sweep of the river and the spectrum in the mist above the falls which had battered him. (3-4)

As he looked at the changes that had occurred to his bit of land, the world political arena, and Osages during his lifetime, he sought to understand the reasons for these changes. This, then, is the inverse of a method of interpretation that first comes up with an overarching scheme and then fits data into that scheme.

As Mathews looks at the various political, cultural, and religious achievements of humans in the context of the environment in which he was living, he is fascinated but not much impressed. Humans, he argues, are living in a period in which they have learned that they are not completely bound by the primal urges and laws of progression—in short, that they have *some* freedom of agency—but that human freedom is neither as complete nor as desirable as humans might like to believe.

The immediate importance of what Mathews achieves is his ability to discuss American Indian religious ecology without slipping into sentimental romanticism. By focusing on the land itself and specific practices relating to it, Mathews opens up both the social-religious world of Osage tradition and Euro-American theology and politics. Throughout, Mathews refuses to separate life-forms from one another in their processes through life and their intentions, motivations, and "ornamentation."

Having set out these presuppositions, in a much more direct fashion than does Mathews, we can see with some clarity his interpretation of what he observed in and around the Blackjacks. The difference between the Osage way of living with the land and that of the invading Euro-Americans was a difference not so much between primitive people and advanced people, but between people who channeled their ornamentation urge toward balance with nature and those who, disastrously, considered the freedom of ornamentation to be a release from natural processes. Articulating these differences in this manner plays itself out in several ways for Mathews and has important ramifications for how we read *Sundown* and evaluate his contribution to our understanding of the challenge of contemporary American Indian existence and survival.

Expressing the ornamentation urge by separation from the primal laws, according to Mathews, results in a lack of long-term thinking that is disastrous both environmentally and socially. One example Mathews gives is the equipment and open pits left by oil exploration crews on his land. As a result, "some of the spots have been barren of vegetation for twenty-five years" (189). The only reason anyone came to clean up the mess was to sell the scrap metal to the Japanese; "The old, rusted boiler that stood near the dry hole for years was like a wart on the prairie; a sore that would not be healed" (189).

Mathews's white neighbor often used the boiler as a pit into which he would cruelly throw live coyote pups. Mathews, after observing this for several years, asked the man, "You know what you have done, . . . you and the cattle and the Jap[anese]? As long as that old boiler was there with your coyotes in it, the cattle came there, smelled the blood, stamped around it, and bawled, like cattle do. They loosened the soil, killed the few weeds and buffalo grass, and started erosion. That wash started. Then they came for the boiler to send to the Japs, and since there was nothing to hold the soil, the ravine started" (189-90). Though there is something of a coyote trickster story in this upbraiding, Mathews points out how one small act, which his neighbor would never think about, could change a part of the landscape.

Mathews normally illustrates this lack of long-term thinking in his several references to the effect of nonindigenous animals, whether human or nonhuman, on the balance of an environment such as the Osage. In some cases this invasion is accounted for and adjusted to within the balance, as in the case of crows and coyotes, who "did agitate the balance when the white [people] came with [their] plows and flocks" (200). The new situation "increased their food supply . . . they adjusted themselves to mechanism with such perfection that it seemed like reasoning" (200).

Other cases, however, did not have such happy results. The English sparrow, he notes, was introduced to North America in 1850 and "now overruns every city from coast to coast" (151). It and other nonindigenous species "burst like steam from a safety valve in America, where their enemies were absent and their food supply abundant" (151).

Only later, in a chapter on the middle of winter, does Mathews interpret these observations and compare them to the global situation. Until January, or "Single Moon By Himself," Mathews seems mainly concerned with describing various hunting trips, encounters with old Osages, and day-to-day life at the sandstone house, with its yard filled with dogs, chickens, birdhouses, and the predators these animals drew (210). January, Mathews says, was when old Osages used to sit around and think about the rest of the year and about the way the world works. "The picture I shall always remember of Single Moon by Himself," Mathews says, "is cold fog and eternal dripping" (210). The weather during that part of the year is not good for hunting, and most household chores can wait until more cheery times, so he spends his time sitting in a chair by the fire reading, at his typewriter writing, or listening to the radio.

Because this is the month when Mathews brings together the experiences of the rest of the book, it is crucial for our study. For the present discussion, we see during Single Moon by Himself the culmination of Mathews's growing critique of Euro-American culture. He compares the arrival of Europeans to North America to the arrival of the sparrow. "Study first the original conditions, wherein Indian[s] [were] in harmony with the natural balance," he says.

> Then study the effect of European[s] freed from the tight political, economic, and social pressures of Europe, running almost berserk on the new continent. [Their] enemies in the Old World were these pressures, and [they were] suddenly freed from them in the New World, to expand even as the English sparrow has. (227)

His contemporaries who were calling for international peace, he went on to argue, continued to be guided by the same desire to separate themselves from the natural laws of progression rather than by their avowed ideology of world brotherhood and sisterhood. Any such peace, Mathews believed, would only be the imposition of power by virile national units over those from whom they were drawing life force (228-30).

The truth behind the balance-of-power politics of his day, as Mathews saw it, was that the powerful countries refused to recognize the inequality involved in international relations. These relationships were relatively new and so far had only been an international extension of the arrogant and destructive ornamentation through which Anglos had created the dust bowl and caused the disappearance of the buffalo. Because these changes had happened without regard for the balance of the environment, they required even more mechanisms of change to protect them from the forces seeking to adjust.

He illustrates this, in his musing by the January fire, by imagining what would happen if the protective mechanisms of Euro-Americans were removed suddenly from the prairie. In the three paragraphs in which he considers which contemporary species would have any chance of survival in such a situation, he mentions "white" species—chickens and cattle—seven times and gives them no chance to survive unless they make major adjustments (230-31).

This focus on "whiteness," which parallels his critique of his white Euro-American political contemporaries, begins very early in the book, when Mathews notices how out of place a pile of white bones from a dead horse is on the prairie (5). In several places he notices from afar a white object.[22] Because of the attention they draw to themselves, Mathews observes, white species require tremendous protection if they are not to be killed by predators.

Without human mechanisms such as fences, guns, and feeding troughs, the white cattle would either adjust quickly or die out. To adjust, their numbers would reduce, as well as their meaty bulk. "This must be done," Mathews imagines, "before the buffalo wolves would come back in numbers. . . . I think also that nature would do something about their glaring white faces, not only for protection against their enemies, but as protection against the sun and pink-eye" (231).

Mathews ends the discussion of what this destructive protectiveness might mean for the Blackjacks after he is dead by saying:

> As long as my ridges in their present condition of balance and comparative peace are of economic benefit to [humans] as profitable grazing range, then my passing will make little difference; but if some foul dough-belly, chewing an unlit cigar and squinting his eyes, decides that there would be greater economic benefit in dividing my pasture into town lots, with a belching factory chimney as the Gothic tower of the religion of mechanism, in the center, the peace of the blackjacks would be destroyed. And the people would talk of a miracle, too, as the earth under which I had been laid would boil with my subterranean writhings. (232)

More than any American Indian writer up to his time and until Deloria, Mathews saw through the presuppositions of the culture that had come to dominate both the land and the people of this continent, and was able to speak with great power about the destructive defects of it.

The way Mathews understood his world at the Blackjacks provides an important perspective on the novel *Sundown*. Deloria's analyses of many of the same issues provide another piece of the critical puzzle.

Deloria on Land and Community

> Indians are like the weather. Everyone knows all about the weather, but none can change it. When storms are predicted, the sun shines. When picnic weather is announced, the rain begins. Likewise, if you count on the unpredictability of Indian people, you will never be sorry.
>
> One of the finest things about being an Indian is that people are always interested in you and your "plight." Other groups have difficulties, predicaments, quandaries, problems, or troubles. Traditionally we Indians have had a "plight."
>
> Our foremost plight is our transparency. People can tell just by looking at us what should be done to help us, how we feel, what a "real" Indian is really like. Indian life, as it relates to the real world, is a continuous attempt not to disappoint people who know us. Unfulfilled expectations cause grief and we have already had our share.

This quotation, from the first page of *Custer Died for Your Sins*, by Vine Deloria Jr., began what has become the most sustained and widest-ranging critique of Western culture by any writing American Indian intellectual.[23] With the appearance of *Custer Died for Your Sins* in 1969, Deloria quickly established himself as one of the brightest, wittiest, and most insightful writers to emerge from the convulsive 1960s.

His work from that period ranges from popular, mainstream books and articles intended to make immediate impact on public attitudes toward Indian affairs to essays for small journals. Throughout, Deloria's sense of humor and wit carry his work. In contrast to the years Mathews spent laboring over ideas about the "roaring stream of civilization," Deloria's work from the late 1960s and 1970s grew from direct engagement with the watershed events that were happening around him.

Though their works grow from radically different moments, Deloria and Mathews are similar in having produced work that finds no natural academic critical audience. In Deloria's case, most theologians are uncomfortable with his work because of his insistence on following religious questions through to what he sees as their logical extreme, even if doing so means calling for an abandonment of any semblance of Christian orthodoxy. Secular thinkers cannot help but

be uncomfortable with Deloria's insistence that religious phenomena have a basis in spiritual reality rather than in human psychology.
He shares the enigmatic status of Mathews—not fitting into any
genre or academic discipline.

In interpreting Deloria's writing, then, we cannot look for the
subtle literary points of *Talking to the Moon*. The rhetorical strategies
and keen eye for tactical writing that he displays, however, make his
work from that watershed period formidable and complex. By his
interweaving of careful analysis, concern for how the work would
impact specific situations, and forceful argument for a generational,
long view of what was happening around him, Deloria displays the
concern of his peers in the 1960s for both short-term pragmatism
and long-term vision.

Ironically, this heat-of-the-moment commentary gives emphasis
to specific historical events, although a central feature of Deloria's
work is the importance of regaining a sense of space and environment in the midst of time. This lack of spatial sense is in fact the
major problem Deloria finds with Christianity and Western culture.
God Is Red, Deloria's fullest theological statement, is first and foremost about time and place.[24] Written at the climax of early 1970s
American Indian activism, it briefly analyzes the current American
Indian political scene, but its main focus is his deepest theological
analysis and critique.

To understand the depth of *God Is Red* is to understand the strategy Deloria uses in it. For those expecting traditional theological
rhetoric or standard academic discourse about American Indian religions, the book is something of a disappointment, because Deloria
asks questions that are different from those that others of his time
and this are asking. He says in an early chapter, "We cannot, of
course, pretend to give an exhaustive answer to any particular question or to present a final definition of either Indian tribal religions
or traditional Christian ideas. What is important is that *alternative
methods of asking questions* or of viewing the world may arise" (89;
emphasis added).

This statement reveals, more than any other, the approach Deloria uses in the book and explains at least in part why a critic like
Andrew Wiget finds that Deloria's work relies on "sweeping gener-
alizations, . . . factual inaccuracies, . . . and doubtful premises."[25]

Most often, the generalized statements Deloria makes come from his desire to proceed to what he sees as more important, fundamental questions that few people are asking. To read simply these comparisons of a generalized Christianity and a generalized American Indian religious perspective is to invite frustration. In each instance Christianity and the political culture that derives from it are found severely wanting and American Indian traditions are shown to be superior. These sections, unfortunately, are the ones that have been of most interest to theologians and critics.[26]

One example among many is Deloria's comments about creation. "Christians," Deloria argues, "see creation as the beginning event of a linear time sequence in which a divine plan is worked out, the conclusion of the sequence being an act of destruction bringing the world to an end" (91). This linear sequence leading ultimately to destruction, he contends, is wrapped up in the notion of fallen, corrupted humanity. In distinction to this, Deloria says later, "For many Indian tribal religions the whole of creation was good, and since the creation event did not include a 'fall,' the meaning of creation was that all parts of it functioned together to sustain it" (95).

Such statements, of course, reduce both Christianity and various American Indian traditions into monoliths. It is not in these reductive comparisons that we find Deloria's real strength. Rather, we find his most important analyses in the fundamental questions that lurk, in his estimation, behind traditional theological questions. These fundamental questions, throughout *God Is Red*, derive from what Deloria sees as Christianity's lack of a relationship to land. Like Mathews, he argues that ecological, political, and spiritual crises of the twentieth century are the result of the misguided attempt to separate humanity from the rest of creation while maintaining a relationship to a god who acts in experienced history. Unlike Mathews, Deloria focuses on Christianity and the Western European and Euro-American culture that derives from it.[27]

As it works itself out in *God Is Red*, this argument begins with a discussion of the Christian concept of history. "When the domestic ideology is divided according to American Indian and Western European immigrant, . . . the fundamental difference is one of great importance," he says (75). This difference is between a place-centered American Indian religious experience and a time-centered

Western European Christianity that is a "steady progression of basically good events and experiences, thereby placing history—time—in the best possible light. . . . Western European peoples have never learned to consider the nature of the world discerned from a spatial point of view" (76).

Deloria does not criticize Christianity for having the *wrong* conception of history. Rather, the point of *God Is Red* is to argue that *any* time-centered religious, philosophical, or political system is problematic. "Time," as he puts it, "has an unusual limitation. It must begin and end at some real points, or it must be conceived as cyclical in nature, endlessly allowing the repetitions of patterns of possibility. Judgment inevitably intrudes into the conception of religious reality whenever a temporal definition is used" (83). Because of this, a sense of place cannot simply be added to time-centered systems. "If time becomes our primary consideration," he argues, "we never seem to arrive at the reality of our existence in places, but are always directed to experiential interpretations rather than to the experiences themselves" (85). This notion is crucial for all of Deloria's criticism; one of the problems of the modern condition is its loss of the impulse to seek direct, unmediated religious experience.

The basic problem with Christianity for Deloria, then, is its subsuming of place by a time-centered theology. In this it completed the movement away from what remained of space-centered theology in post-Exilic Judaism. Following the apocalyptic trends of their time, the followers of Jesus after his death developed a theology that "looks toward a spectacular end of the world as a time of judgment and thus an end of history" (119). Rather than a god who acts in history with a specific group of people in a specific place, Christianity became one universal version of what had been at one time a religion tied to Palestine—its people and places.

The Jesus movement's response to the question of how people could retain their integrity after losing their land base to Rome was, initially, akin to that of other apocalyptic movements. As Deloria says, "The immediate followers who had known Jesus had come to the conclusion . . . that their Lord would return within their own lifetime to restore the Kingdom of Israel to the glory known during the eras of David and Solomon" (118). When this did not happen, the early Christians had to come up with a new ideology that would retain the central belief in "a spectacular end of the world" but that would also provide a way to continue living while Christians waited (119). Thus came the idea, "with the establishment of the organizational Church as a political power in the crumbling Roman Empire . . . the temporary doctrine that Jesus had established a 'church' to supervise the affairs of [humans] until he decided to return" (120).

In universalizing its past experience in the particular place of Palestine, he says, "the reality of religion . . . becomes its ability to explain the universe, not experience it. Creeds and beliefs replace apprehension of whatever relationship may exist with higher powers" (79). Further, along with providing no basis for actually experiencing life in the world, temporal-centered Christianity can no longer, in the twentieth century, even provide a sure foundation of knowing when and where the Christian god acts in time.

Unlike the vast majority of his nonfundamentalist contemporaries, Deloria makes an assumption that religious stories and myths do not spring from the human imagination, but from "*Something* . . . observed or experienced by a community. . . . The basic myth may be refined to some extent, but it is not subject to very much editing" (84). Because Christianity removes itself from place and, concomitantly, experience, it is able to dismiss myths and stories to the realm of pure imagination. "Temporal theologians," he says, "place great reliance on the poetic imagination as the source of religious imagination" (84).

Having construed his argument in this way, Deloria points out what he sees as the great irony of modern Christianity. On the one hand, he says, Christian theology developed in such a way as to give universal primacy to a set of events that supposedly provides the evidence of how and where the Christian god acts in history. On the other hand, liberal Christians, for the most part, have reduced their most important stories—Exodus and Easter—to inspirational folklore and primitive imagination.

After reviewing the work of some Christian theologians of his time, including Harvey Cox and Louis Dupré, who were looking to the Exodus and Easter for their relevant message of hope and social change, Deloria makes this point forcefully. He shows how Dupré speaks quite eloquently about the Exodus, then adds in a footnote,

"obviously in all this I do not take a position on the historical character of this event or of any particular miracle" (136). To this, Deloria reacts as follows:

> Can this be? Can Christian theologians tell us that their
> God works in and dominates history while maintaining in
> their footnotes that they are not prepared to affirm that any-
> thing really happened? What about the resurrection? What
> kind of body did Jesus actually have? A "glorified" body? Or
> the body in which he walked on earth? Are Christian thinkers
> prepared to say? . . .
> If the major events of the Bible are to be taken not as actual
> events involving [people], events of such significance that they
> could be used later as patterns by which the subsequent
> "church" could discern God dropping "hints" in the affairs of
> men, then what do we make of the Christian religion? Can we
> take it seriously? Even more, can we affirm that it is superior to
> any other religion, and if so, on what basis? . . .
> Christians ask us to accept that there is a history, that there
> is a central event making the rest of the history intelligible, and
> that because there is a central event, there must necessarily be
> a history. The logic is clearly a precursor to *Catch-22*. When-
> ever we focus on one of the very important events of that line
> of history, we are told by Protestants, Roman Catholics, and
> Jews alike that what happened was really just the growth of
> legend, folklore, and glorification, not a spectacular event.
> (136-37)

From here, Deloria forces home the point. "The dilemma over the
nature of history occurs and will occur wherever a religion is divorced from space and made an exclusive agent of time. Events become symbolic teaching devices, and the actual sequence of events
becomes unimportant" (137).[28] Temporal-centered Christianity,
then, insists on having its cake and eating it, too: a "religion should
. . . never back off and disclaim . . . the historical nature of [an]
event . . . while becoming furious with other people for not believing its claim" (138).

Deloria will not countenance the defense often made by Christians that "one cannot judge Christianity by the actions of Western
secular" people (127). Rather than engaging in esoteric arguments

about the relationship of "Christ and culture" or "Church and society," he repeats again and again the historical record of the past two thousand years. He shows the presence and the influence of the Christian Church throughout the development of Western imperialist ideologies and puts the burden of proof on Christians to show why they are not "inseparable" from that history (127). He echoes Roan Horse's speech in *Sundown*—those who want to find out now how to fix the theology and the damage have arrived too late.

Such analytical strategies produce even more trenchant comments in Deloria's discussion of community and human personality. Throughout his writing he argues against the possibility of understanding human existence and building community with a theology that is temporal-centered. As he does in his more general discussion of land, he refers to early Christianity in discussing the devastating effects the subsuming of place has for communities and individuals.

Christianity, Deloria reiterates, has its origins in the expectation of the return of Jesus, a time-bound notion, to his followers in Palestine and the theological adjustments early Christians had to make when the return of Jesus was not immediately forthcoming. This waiting for a temporal event "is extremely important in understanding the nature of the Christian conception of the human personality, because it indicates that the various theories were fundamentally accommodations to the incidents in the life of the early Christian community and not intended to reflect a reasoned, mature, or even rational understanding of human beings" (190).

Further, what began as one expression within Judaism as to the religious destiny of Palestine would proceed "with the theological speculations of Paul far beyond its original intent or scope" (192). Paul's cosmic interpretation of the meaning of Jesus Christ for the world eventually became divorced from its apocalyptic roots, and "Christianity gained political control over the lives of Western [people] . . . and . . . many of its original premises continue to exert influence over the way [people] think about themselves, especially in the field of religious experiences" (192).

What remains of the earlier sectarian apocalyptic message in the cosmic interpretation of Christianity, Deloria contends, is the emphasis on preaching, repentance, and conversion. Theologically, the goal of early Christianity was to prepare the nation of Israel for the return of their Messiah and an anticipated dawning of a new age of national sovereignty. Within such a system, "conversion and salvation doctrines are dependent on the exercise of individual will to achieve certain standards of behavior or to make a record with respect to good and evil deeds" (195-96).

Deloria then moves on to argue that such a system may sound fine at the speculative level but cannot provide a foundation for living adequate to the needs of human experience. He shows this at two levels. First, in attempting to impose a set of standards of behavior, this set of standards "eventually falls victim to cultural values" (196). He points to several historical examples of what he sees as cultural determination of Christian values, including monogamy and divorce and poverty and wealth (196-97).

The other observation he makes is that individualism is a natural requirement of traditional, ancient Christian doctrine:

> In terms of philosophical analysis, what Christian doctrines purport to do is to isolate the individual human being in a vacuum where [she or] he is confronted with a deity who is, by definition, angry. Every consideration [she or] he could conceivably make, based on [her or] his relationships with the world of daily experience, are negated as factors to be considered as part of [her or] his religious experience. [She or] he is then asked to make a theoretical choice on whether certain factual happenings on this planet indicated a radical change of cosmic significance to the deity. Upon giving [her or] his assent, [she or] he must exercise [her or] his will to prevent the commission of further disobedience toward the deity when [she or] he faces the world of daily experience. Then [she or] he is once again placed in that world and expected to respond to novel situations in a manner consistent with the concept of obedience to divine commands and purposes which remain obscured if not invisible to [her or] him. (199)

Thus, the time-bound effects of Christian doctrine are to move individuals toward highly specific systems of obedience and disobedience and away from community.

As he moves to his discussion of the Christian concept of community, the inability of Christian theology to bear these criticisms becomes abundantly and powerfully clear. Consistent with other doctrines, he argues, early Christians redefined community as not existing in a particular place, but in a time not yet present. "This . . . began," he says, "as Paul developed his theology and the subsequent doctrines of creation, history, and atonement. . . . In opening the religion to the Gentiles, the whole conception of a Chosen People was radically changed from an identifiable group or nation to a mysterious conglomeration of people who could not be identified with any degree of accuracy" (211-12). By defining the Church as the body of Christ, "no one knew or could know who belonged to it until the final judgment, when everything would be revealed" (212). The Church could claim on one hand, Deloria argues, that God would sort out the real Christians from the false ones at the end of time while on the other hand its leaders rose to positions of power in which they sanctioned decisions in the name of God.

Within such a conception of an invisible and a visible Church, Deloria points out,

> It . . . becomes virtually impossible to discuss the conception of religious community, . . . since no visible community can or does exist. Any efforts to identify failures with any of the religious denominations brings the response that the particular denomination in question is not really the Church. . . . The tendency among Christian theologians is . . . to speak as if the denomination were in fact the Church that exists invisibly and sinlessly off stage. (216-17)

Deloria contrasts this concept of community with what he finds among American Indian tribal groups. Within these groups, he says, "Tribal members know who they are, and for better or worse the whole tribe is involved in its relations with the rest of the world" (219).

This does not mean, however, that everyone within the group agrees or sees the world in the same way. Even if they split up into factions, though, the groups retain responsibility for everyone in them. In contrast to the Christian propensity to disclaim the actions of some Christians, Deloria states that among American Indians "no one will reject a tribal member as not belonging to the tribe. He may be viciously attacked as corrupt, as having assimilated, or as being a stupid traditional. He is never disclaimed as a tribal member" (220).

Because it cannot identify its true membership and can disassociate itself from any feature it finds distasteful, Deloria says, Christianity is missing "the self-critical mechanism for analyzing behavior" (220).

What we find in Deloria's critique of Christianity and the West is an unrelenting refusal to allow white Christians in the United States to speak of themselves as separate from the U.S. political economy. This comes in various ways, but the questions he was asking in 1971 are the same as those he has asked in more recent work: "Does not the American understanding of social and world reality really derive from and depend upon the Christian theological and metaphysical understanding of the world to such a degree that America would not make sense aside from this context?"[29]

Most theologians working then and now were attempting to ferret out troubling questions of how it is that the Church relates to society and were worried that the dynamics of social existence had invaded the Church, but Deloria's intent has been to contend that such questions are at best unrealistic and at worst ridiculous. As in his analysis of the category of land, he places the burden of proof in this instance on Christian theology and asks where the self-critical and identifying categories are, so that people outside of the Church can know with some surety with whom and with what they are dealing.

Posing the question of Christ and culture in this way puts Christians in a defensive position in which the burden of proof lies with them as to why we should not regard the history of the United States as an obvious outgrowth of Christianity rather than as two discrete units that can be isolated from each other. More than anything else for Deloria, this lack of identifiable, self-critical communities reveals the inadequacy of traditional orthodox Christianity to respond to contemporary existence. The Christian tradition, he argues, "is inadequate, because it has not reached any fundamental problems: it is only a patch and paste job over . . . serious theological problem[s]" (98).

Overcoming this time-centered, nonexperiential approach to understanding religious experience, Deloria says, requires modern humans to give up their assumption that because of human progress they now know more about the world than did people in the past.

The time orientation of both Western science and Western theology, he argues, "overlooks the uniqueness of spiritual power in the effort to demythologize everything; to say that almost everything that happened didn't really happen because we don't experience it now."[30] This leads him to a discussion about critical issues that arise in a return to religious traditions that are place-centered.

The question of traditions for Deloria goes beyond finding psychoanalytic or anthropological explanations or even a primary concern with their social function. In discussing the Lakota story of how the sacred pipe was brought to the people by white buffalo calf woman, Deloria asks, "Did some Indian make that up thousands of years ago? And if he [or she] did, how did he [or she] convince all the subsequent generations of Indians that it really happened?" He does not accept that such things develop from "the tiny seed of an idea which is elaborated upon and refined by a series of poets and preachers."[31]

Deloria is willing to go so far as to say that "the intensity of the events, and some of the specifics, [are] lost as time goes by," but he clearly advocates throughout his work that contemporary people move out of the realm of psychology into actual events in order to understand the power of these Native traditions.[32] Respect for traditions, on Deloria's reading, requires approaching them without pejoratively assuming that they are the products of simpleminded people who are easily duped.

What is of crucial importance here is Deloria's recognizing the necessity, as does Mathews, of overcoming what amounts to a theological assumption that tribal people live an ossified, unchanging existence until crossing a line into dynamic existence. This allows both Mathews and Deloria to do two things. First, it opens up the continuity between American Indian experience before contact with Europeans and after. Both are clear in saying that the situation in which American Indian people find themselves is radically different from that before contact, but to manufacture a fallen nature is to slip into Western, Christian assumptions.

Second, by pointing out that these traditions were and are in process allows both writers to discuss the power of those traditions in material, rather than ideal, terms. Deloria consistently points out the material ways these traditions have led to actual experience. For instance, he describes the disciplined method by which Osages would decide when to return to harvest their gardens in what is now Missouri after a summer's hunt in the Rockies. "In the middle of July [Osages] would begin to examine one of the mountain flowers and when this flower began to turn to seed they would know it was time. . . . Such a task required that the Osage know the relationships of plants, animals, and lands over a distance of 1,000 miles."[33]

This is one of many examples of how a "remarkable system of relationships undergirds a seemingly innocent life . . . [that] deal[s] with specific relationships between specific individuals."[34] Along with an openness to the spiritual power of the land, he continues, Native traditions require intense amounts of disciplined study and wide experience. The goal of that discipline is to move toward maturity, the same state that Mathews points toward.

Deloria remarks on maturity in an essay on the work of Paul Feyerabend, the antimethodological English philosopher. Deloria praises Feyerabend for his advocacy of a paradigm shift not based in Thomas Kuhn's belief that "novices" in established institutions of knowledge (e.g., academic science) provide the impetus for significant change. Feyerabend argues instead that those outside of those institutions have the sort of knowledge needed to come up with new ways of dealing with the world. And it is those mature forms of neglected knowledge that are the most important. Deloria contends that maturity is exactly the goal of American Indian epistemologies.[35]

He points out that he has been saying similar things throughout his career but that "the reception which non-Western thinker[s] receive is frequently one of paternalism, more often a chiding ridicule that a native would presume to enter the lists of educated people, and occasionally a deep jealousy and resentment when the non-Westerner appears to have something important to say to the Western scheme of things."[36] In another context he says of his work that he has attempted to "raise suspicions in the minds of people that maybe there is another way of looking at things. Changing the framework within which logics and concepts exist will make it considerably easier to create changes in legal and political status."[37]

Deloria's work provides a way of viewing Mathews's categories as set forth in *Talking to the Moon*. We find in Deloria the same impulse to find new ways to discuss human experience as we do in

Mathews. Both figures recognize that the process of moving toward maturity remains open and are critical of any praxis that has people simply waiting around for an outside agency to change their status.

This, finally, was what perplexed Mathews about what he perceived as the strategy of the full-blood Osages at the turn of the century, his contention that they were refusing to move forward. In spite of his long view of history, he did not recognize that in their resistance they were making possible their reemergence many decades later. Mathews's failure to recognize this is ironic because his own interpretive scheme leads to that conclusion. In other words, the Chal Windzers of one generation can create the possibilities for the next generation.

Deloria proceeds from the hope for possibility to the creation of possibility. Rather than remaining stunted in moving from virility toward maturity, Deloria's work is a prime example, intellectually, of recognizing limits and possibilities for action and then going forward. At the same time he recognizes that those possibilities exist in the midst of constantly new challenges. As we see clearly in *Sundown*, no matter how resilient the full-blood noncooperationists were, many people in the community were succumbing to the pressures of the oppressive situation. Having now teased out some of the critical contours of *Talking to the Moon* and *God Is Red*, we begin to see *Sundown* from a new perspective.

That new perspective is vital to understanding the culture whose values gain a firmer foothold every day in American Indian communities. However attractive Deloria and Mathews make the traditional conceptions of land and community, American Indian communities today live with the influences and confluences of both traditional and Western culture. In developing a critical stance toward those destructive values, what is at stake for American Indian communities in confronting the challenge of maintaining tradition and building community becomes more and more clear.

Sundown Revisited

Sundown seems quite a different novel after looking at it with the insights gained from Deloria and Mathews. Instead of a tragic victim and a community caught in the battle between an either/or of assimilation or remaining traditional, we see the real problem—a community having severely limited ability to make choices regarding its own future and the effect of that on a typical individual within the community. This is why linking Chal's education to the Osage political situation is of utmost importance. Chal's identity problems begin when he goes away to the predominantly white private school, but this event is linked closely with the abrogation of the Osage Nation's sovereign council.

Even the most cursory understanding of Mathews's thoughts in *Talking to the Moon* provides a deeper way of reading *Sundown* than the interpretations discussed at the beginning of this chapter. Recall the major themes of the novel: Chal spends his whole life waiting for something to happen that will allow him to fully express himself. On the night when he does his drunken, solo dance, he cannot express the emotion that is "dammed up within him." He wants to "strut about before an enemy . . . and declare to the silent world about him that he [is] a glorious male." Most obviously, he talks about his desire to have an "orgasm [climax] of the spirit," which he is unable to have. He ends the scene by looking with frustration at the blackjacks because they are so "patient."

Mathews alludes to interrupted virility in *Talking to the Moon* when he says, "The species of my ridges that do not attain their climaxes remain intensely virile and await the inevitable decline of the senile, no matter how long they must wait, and virility remains always a 'danger' to senility" (230). Further, we can see Chal's awakening to these feelings at the moment of the abrogation of Osage self-determined government and his going to the predominantly Anglo school as an interruption in his stage of virility. As Mathews says of interrupted virility, though, it does not just die or remain dormant. We see in Chal a prime example of the intensity of interrupted virility. Having lived during the period when the United States still recognized, however reluctantly, the fullness of Osage sovereignty, Chal internalized the maturing values that sovereignty allows. The ways various characters express that intensity indicate how Mathews judged the various political strategies of the time. The mixed-blood Progressives, he indicates, failed because their self-hate inspired denial of the tradition that would keep them moored to the land.

The full-bloods stay moored to the culture but put themselves in tremendous danger by doing so. Roan Horse's speech is a partial vindication of the noncooperationist strategy, but Mathews also points to the large number of full-bloods who have committed suicide, have become dependent on drugs and alcohol, or have been taken advantage of because they did not have a nuanced enough relationship to those dominating them.[38]

This reading, then, draws from *Sundown* meanings and nuances that the traditional critical categories of alienation, tragedy, and unredeemed suffering cannot. Using them promotes a view of American Indian history that highlights decline, inevitable disintegration of the legal and political status of tribal nations, and Western superiority. Mathews, as this reading argues, has gone to great lengths to counter these categories with his own interpretation of Chal's life. At the end, when Chal considers law school, Mathews has put into his mind one way through which he can reach out in his virility to establish power over some corner of the life force. Though it may be a small step, it is a means of survival and signals the possibility for Chal to continue the patient, frustrating struggle of waiting for the dominant life-forms of his environment to reach their climax and then pass into senility.

In *Sundown* the situation is dire, but not tragic in the way of McNickle's *The Surrounded*. Archilde, the protagonist of that work, is sober, motivated, and seeks to do something to escape his difficult situation. The deterministic message of the early McNickle seems to be one of ultimate despair. However much this attitude is warranted by the situation of McNickle's day, Mathews provides not so much an alternative as the possibility of an alternative. Drawing his lessons not just from the outlines of one person's life, but also from the land and from the resiliency of a community committed to resistance, Mathews offers a way to exercise what power of decision making is available, limited though the positive effect may be.

In the end, the question of whether or not Chal goes to law school is more important for its asking than for its answering. For if Chal does not go to law school and chooses instead to continue in dissipated drunkenness, others like him will indeed make the choice to survive and wait out the inevitable decline of the species that has invaded their environment and interrupted their growth through virility to climax and maturity. As long as some Osages are willing to exercise their virility for survival, the tribe has a future.

Deloria's analyses of land and community further bolster this reading. Like Mathews, he seeks to understand American Indian traditions in light of a great number of economic, religious, social, political, and biological factors. In *Sundown* and *Talking to the Moon* we see examples of the political and spiritual battle of which Deloria speaks in *God Is Red*. In both writers' works, traditionalism, religious ecology, political resistance, and the integrity of communities coexist in a crucible of experience in which none can be forgotten. Unlike Mathews, Deloria believes that Native traditions are a necessary part of the struggle for American Indian sovereignty. Mathews shows persuasively, though, that the battle rages as much internally as externally and cannot be reduced to a mere us-versus-them.

In advocating his position Deloria says that returning to tradition must be part of a multilayered process of change. Central to this process is a recognition that "religious forms must, in order to be meaningful, relate to a dramatically changed community in a dramatically changed environment."[39] When it became apparent that tradition was going to become a force in American Indian politics, he said,

> I believe that when the traditionalists realize that the basis of Indian tribal religions is not preserving social forms and ceremonies but creating new forms and ceremonies to confront new situations, they will have an extremely promising future. Many tribal religions have their roots in the distant past, but took on their present forms little more than a century before the coming of the white[s].
>
> Unlike many other religious traditions, tribal religions . . . have not been authoritatively set "once and for always." Truth is in the ever changing experiences of the community. For the traditional Indian to fail to appreciate this aspect of [her or] his heritage is the saddest of heresies. It means the Indian has unwittingly fallen into the trap of Western religion, which seeks to freeze history in an unchanging and authoritative past.[40]

This was written in the aftermath of Wounded Knee in 1973, when Deloria saw a great danger in holding up the symbols, rhetoric, and trappings of Native traditions without coming to a critical position as to what possible material benefits local communities could gain from the neotraditional move and what actual structures—political, religious, social, both internal and external to communities—stand in the way.

In these remarks Deloria indicates that Natives need to stand in the same sort of existential dilemma that Chal Windzer is in at the end of *Sundown*. Chal's awakened consciousness and affirmation of tradition upon hearing the words of Roan Horse and seeing the subtle actions of his mother are similar to what happened in the early 1970s around Native America. But both Mathews and Deloria contend that this affirmation and raised consciousness, however necessary, are not the end point of the process.

For both, land and community are necessary starting points for the process of coming to a deep perception of the conflicts and challenges that face American Indian people and communities. They take into account the various groups of people, Native and non-Native, whose choices and actions influence a situation as well as the historical and biological backdrop-in-process that also has its influence. To fail to find a way of keeping these many factors in place, especially the ones internal to Native communities, is to fall easily into romantic excesses regarding Native traditions.

Deloria and Mathews are examples of intellectuals who were able to take many factors into account and who provide a general framework for approaching critical issues. Both recognized that the silence of the traditional people was not due to their having nothing to say. They also saw that those who were speaking most loudly could be, and often have been, wrongheaded and misguided.

As presented in the previous chapter, the factors that now present themselves to a full and inclusive understanding of contemporary Indian life have changed considerably since Mathews and Deloria wrote *Talking to the Moon* and *God Is Red*. Importantly, though, engaging Mathews's portrayal of Chal's unnamed Osage mother in *Sundown* or his characterization of the feminine in *Talking to the Moon* does not necessitate a dismissal of what he wrote. Rather, his perspective invites a discussion of how the work would have been different had he been more inclusive. That invitation derives from his commitment to understanding biological and social life as a process rather than as an entity that bears the marks of some essence. His approach, then, is open not only to change, but to reorientation. The same is true of Deloria. Because he speaks of tradition in an open-ended way, new factors and experiences can fit into his framework.

My literary critical strategy here has been to read across the texts of Deloria and Mathews and highlight the ways in which that reading across opens up the texts of each. The literary description of a community in crises of land and sovereignty that Mathews provides in *Sundown*, I have argued, deepens our historical sense of that moment and the rest of the past one hundred years. By reading *Sundown* in this way, I have hoped to demonstrate that relying either on standard critical categories of individual alienation and historically necessary tragedy or on essentializing concepts of radical Otherness severely limits the textual landscapes of Mathews and Deloria. Their process-centered openings-up of American Indian community experiences, in fact, work against the grain of both strategies and defy any containing and constricting reading. They challenge us, as critical readers, to move always toward mature understandings of, as Mathews put it, how the localized roots of a tree move and grow toward its cosmopolitan trunk, branches, and leaves.

That challenge becomes especially important in considering the positionality of American Indian intellectuals facing a contemporary situation in which the influences and confluences of an increasingly complex world stand always on both sides of the border of critical praxis. Indeed, the myriad attractions of contemporary criticism and discourse stand waiting for our critical engagements and responses.

3 / Intellectual Sovereignty and the Struggle for an American Indian Future

John Joseph Mathews and Vine Deloria Jr., as shown in chapter 2, portray the conflict between American Indians and Euro-Americans as one best seen in initial terms of land and community. Both writers point to the process through which the U.S. government abrogated the sovereign-sovereign relationship with Natives as a major turning point in the history of that conflict. The multifaceted battle to appropriate Native land, supplant Native religion, and undermine Native traditional social structures is the mise-en-scène of American Indian intellectual work of the past one hundred years. Deloria and Mathews keep these various factors in tension as they work to understand both the history of that conflict and what kind of future American Indians might have.

In this chapter I will discuss the issues their analyses raise for contemporary American Indian intellectual work and argue that a process-centered understanding of sovereignty provides a way of envisioning the work Native scholars do. Having established in chapter 1 the intellectual context of Deloria and Mathews and having considered the question of how to read their work in chapter 2, I will turn here to the issues of the role of American Indian intellectuals in the struggle for sovereignty and of how we can make American Indian discourse more inclusive of contemporary American Indian experiences.

I will set the stage for that discussion by looking at Deloria's and Mathews's conceptions of how American Indians can face the challenge of asserting sovereignty. Following this will be a discussion of the centrality of the category of experience for both figures and my argument that both writers' analyses of chaos and maturity present a compelling way of seeing the contemporary situation of American Indian intellectuals. I will conclude this study by turning to one aspect of contemporary American Indian literature, poetry, and demonstrating how the insights gained from this reading of Mathews and Deloria open up that material in crucial ways.

Deloria and the Implicit Recognition of Group Sovereignty

By the time he wrote *God Is Red*, Deloria believed that the key to an American Indian future was the return to Native ceremonies and traditions within a framework of asserting sovereignty. He was certainly not the only American Indian leader making such an appeal. Leaders of the American Indian Movement and others were making efforts to base their political activism in traditional culture, and some of the first tradition-based substance abuse programs were under development. By now, such appeals have become commonplace.

With *God Is Red* Deloria provided the first and much-needed critical reflection on questions raised by such appeals to tradition. Such revitalization, he argued, must take place in the context of a larger framework if it is not, as presented in chapter 2, to slip into dogmatic Western religious assumptions. That framework had remained consistent through a half decade of extremely energetic American Indian activism. As American Indians and other oppressed groups were caught up in the fervor of nationalistic and separatist politics in the early 1970s, Deloria was asking what nationalism, self-determination, and group sovereignty could really mean in the world of lived experience.

The events that led to the takeover of Wounded Knee were a fulfillment of the goals of many leaders of Deloria's generation. At the same time, as argued in chapter 1, these events created a set of problems that represented a realization of the greatest fears of those leaders. When he published *Custer Died for Your Sins* in 1969, Deloria wrote that "Indian people . . . have a chance to re-create a type of society for themselves that can defy, mystify, and educate the rest of

American society." His stated hope was not so much to be right or wrong, but to give a "new sense of conflict to Indian affairs" and to "bring . . . to the surface the greatness that is in" American Indian people and cultures.[1]

The stage was set at that point, he indicated, for the emergence of just that sort of transformation in American Indian communities. National Indian leaders had for over a decade carefully defined an agenda that would take advantage of national attention to minority needs without allowing themselves to be merely lumped together with other minority groups. The treaty-based nationalism of traditional people in isolated reservation communities had begun to have an impact on young leaders in national Indian politics. Diasporic American Indians were mobilizing to bring issues specific to their experience onto the national scene.

Beyond the politics of the moment, Deloria argued, American Indians would eventually have to capitalize on the gains made in the previous decade and solidify the process of American Indian communities' taking control of their own destinies. The time was coming, he predicted, when the politics of confrontation would have to end and the work of building communities would have to begin. Even the conservative turn toward "law and order" prompted by white racist fear of African-American militancy and moralistic fear of drugs and rock and roll was a positive part of the American Indian struggle, insofar as these events were forcing Indians to withdraw into their own communities and draw on their own cultural strength.[2] Deloria was most concerned with four parts of the puzzle that might come together to interrupt this process.

First, he was concerned that the urban-based movement would become embroiled in reservation political battles rather than developing its own agenda, tailor-made to the needs of Natives living in diaspora. Second, he feared that dispossessed Natives would uncritically copy the tactics of Black Power. Third, he warned that media coverage of American Indian activism would turn political struggle into a circus in which activists with the most spectacular rhetoric would be the focus of attention. Finally, he worried that in the midst of all the political activity, people in the Indian movement would fail to think critically and analyze the issues that were arising.[3]

All of these fears were realized between 1969 and 1973. However disappointed Deloria's writings show him to have been in the turns American Indian activism took during that time, he also recognized as much as any of his writing contemporaries the critical importance of those events. First, the various sectors of the grassroots Indian movement confronted the Native establishment with the fact that their reformist tactics did not speak to large numbers of American Indian people on reservations and in urban areas. Second, the militants gravitated with ease toward traditional spiritual leaders very early on, asserting that a truly liberative American Indian politics would have at its center an affirmation of culture, spirituality, and tradition.

Because the militant activists, in contrast to the Native establishment, were able to draw great numbers of people to their ranks, Deloria continued to support their efforts in court and in print. However valid were the charges that the militants were urban gangsters, confrontationists who refused to negotiate, and the "romantic inversion of racialism," they undeniably touched a nerve in the consciousness of American Indian people from the poorest and most alienated of backgrounds.[4]

Even as these events transpired, Deloria grappled with what their actions meant for the future of American Indian sovereignty and freedom. A good example is Deloria's warning to American Indians against copying the tactics of other power movements. He contended that the various nationalist groups of the late 1960s had largely missed the point of what they were demanding. He sets out his criticisms of the militant power movements in, among other places, a chapter of *We Talk, You Listen* called "Power, Sovereignty, and Freedom."[5] He begins the chapter by saying that the concept of power that was sweeping minority groups of the United States needed to be defined clearly because "where it has not been defined, activism has been substituted for power itself" (114). "Few members of racial minority groups," he argues, "have realized that inherent in their peculiar experience on this continent is hidden the basic recognition of their power and sovereignty" (115).

That peculiar experience, he contends, is that the U.S. government, through discrimination and through its historical legislation—its treaties, amendments, or statutes—recognizes the presence of discrete racial, cultural, and religious groups within its borders. The ostensible goal of that explicit acknowledgment, of course, is to somehow violate the integrity of the groups and move them into the mainstream of individual rights. Even though to Deloria this is "a quicksand of assimilationist theories which destroy the power of the group to influence its own future," acknowledgment of group status remains (118).

American Indians, of course, have the strongest footing in this regard because of the existence of parallel institutions in American Indian communities that are federally recognized or have traditional forms of government still in place. Sovereignty, in Deloria's definition, requires constructive group action rather than demands for self-determination, "since power cannot be given and accepted. . . . The responsibility which sovereignty creates is oriented primarily toward the existence and continuance of the group" (123).

The path of sovereignty, he says, is the path to freedom. That freedom, though, is not one that can be immediately defined and lived. Rather, the challenge is to articulate what sort of freedom as it "emerge[s]" through the experience of the group to exercise the sovereignty which they recognize in themselves (124). Through this process-centered definition of sovereignty, Deloria is able to avoid making a declaration as to what contemporary American Indian communities are or are not. Instead, Deloria recognizes that American Indians have to go through a process of building community and that that process will define the future.

What Deloria articulates, then, is a position that does not simply posit the essential superiority of American Indian traditions over other ways of life and cultures. His argument that American Indian traditions are the best way of living arises from the presence of those traditions in this particular place for such a long period of time and from the actual practices derived from them. He also points to many other groups in the United States—the Nation of Islam, the Amish, the Acadians of Louisiana—that have managed to create and sustain a sovereign identity (129, 133).

Deloria is pointedly humanistic in asserting that we must evaluate our situation based on what humans have created and how they have created it. He also advocates a position that is not merely a call for the United States to break down into tribes closed off from the rest of the world. Rather, he recognizes that the withdrawal of a group to draw on its own resources does not cut it off from other groups' influences on its future. And he argues that humans of different cultures need to have the positive experiences of culture affirmation while at the same time they need to confront a set of challenges for which no culture has all answers. Evaluating various perspectives requires speaking of the actual practices and processes involved.

The necessity of discussing sovereignty in terms of actual practices, according to Deloria, comes from confronting a system that abstracts principles in order to impose its will on others. "Can we," he asks, "continue to struggle for justice on an atomistic premise that society is merely a conglomerate of individuals who fall under the same laws?" (106). His answer, of course, is no. Because groups accomplish little by demanding that the dominating society change, Deloria advocates building communities and social structures through which those communities exercise political, economic, and spiritual power along with responsibility.

Yielding to the temptation to lash out at the oppressor, according to Deloria, is to be avoided not for humanistic reasons or to avoid the backlash that such actions produce. Rather, such actions keep the various groups from exercising the power that they already possess, a power, Deloria argues, that is not only the positive material of their cultural and political lives that they have been able to maintain over years of oppression, but also in the "persecution of a group because it is a group" (117).

In coming together to demand self-determination and sovereignty, he says, groups in the 1970s were taking the first steps toward finding an alternative to the false consciousness and praxis of individualism in the United States. What was lacking in these demands, however, was a realization that the dominating society had already acknowledged the existence of the group, even if in doing so it violated its own mythologies of the primacy of individual rights and property ownership.

As Deloria criticized the power movements, he had to recognize the ability of the extreme, nationalist message of militant activists to awaken within American Indians the kind of consciousness through which large numbers of people rise up to take their destinies into their own hands. In the afterword to *Custer Died for Your Sins* he had said that he "want[ed] to search out the sheep missing from our national Indian fold" (278). His goal in doing so would be to "help them get moving with the rest of the tribes" (278). As the actions of the 1970s unfolded, those lost sheep multiplied into the myriad Indian voices, some in the fold, many outside of it, that remain to this day.

The combination of diasporic anger and reservation-based traditional people created tremendous energy that the leaders from NCAI and NIYC had never been able to tap into. Further, to the poorest and least visible American Indians they provided an alternative. Deloria contended that, as the presence of these new voices and experiences grew in number, strength, and vocality, the framework of sovereignty that he had argued for in 1970 was still basically sound. Without this framework, he feared, tradition-based revitalization would not be able to respond adequately to the political, economic, and social necessities of American Indian communities.

The return to tradition, as discussed in chapter 2, cannot in Deloria's analysis be an unchanging and unchangeable set of activities, but must be part of the life of a community as it struggles to exercise its sovereignty. Although dressing up in beads and feathers provided a successful means of gaining media attention and funding from progressives and churches, it did not get at the deeper issues of how viable, responsible communities could emerge in Indian country.

Tradition is limited in this way, he argued, because it was not originally developed to confront the particular challenges of contemporary American Indian communities and politics. A contemporary American Indian politics would have to grapple with a situation that made demands requiring the creation of new categories of existence and experience. He sums this up in an interview:

> Everyone doesn't have to do everything that the old Indians did in order to have a modern Indian identity. We don't have to have every male in the tribe do the Sun Dance. We need a larger variety of cultural expression today. I don't see why Indians can't be poets, engineers, songwriters or whatever. I don't see why we can't depart from traditional art forms and do new things. Yet both Indians and whites are horrified when they learn that an Indian is not following the rigid forms and styles

of the old days. That is nonsense to me but it has great meaning to a lot of people who have never considered the real
meaning of cultural change and national development.[6]

To understand what the "real meaning" of traditional revitalization
is, then, American Indians must realize that the power of those traditions is not in their formal superiority but in their adaptability to
new challenges.

After Wounded Knee, Deloria's criticisms of the militant movement were very pointed even though he supported the action in
court and in print. By then, he felt, the Indian movement had lost
any sense of pragmatism and had replaced its own place-centered
traditions with an "eschatological vision" similar to that of the
Ghost Dance movement eighty-three years earlier. "The movement
of today," he says in comparing the Wounded Knee takeover to the
Ghost Dance movement, "asserts the cultural superiority of Indian
traditions over those of Anglo-Saxon peoples. The inherent superiority will, it is alleged, become historically manifest."[7] In arguing
thus, he continues his warning against falling into the trap of an idealism that loses its sense of pragmatism.

The traditionalist-urban militant movement had not yet decided,
according to Deloria, how it would deal with the new, offensive situation in a way consistent with Indian traditions. Because they had
practiced sovereignty through traditional ceremonies and social relationships, the traditionalists were in a much better position to confront the needs of communities than were the tribal councils, whose
primary interests were short-term and economic.[8] In other words,
the traditionalists represented the emergence of a marginalized perspective that held much promise but was not the answer in and of
itself.

The struggle for freedom, then, could not be a matter simply of
dressing up in the trappings of the past and making demands. Deloria pointed out that those who turn tradition into idols fail to understand the real power of those traditions. "Truth," as previously
quoted, "is in the ever changing experiences of the community. For
the traditional Indian to fail to appreciate this aspect of [her or] his
own heritage is the saddest of heresies. It means the Indian has unwittingly fallen into the trap of Western religion."[9]

To summarize, Deloria's experience as the most prolific commentator on American Indian activism in the early 1970s produced his particular views on the role tradition can and should play in the development of an American Indian future. First, he contended, the affirmation of tradition provides the necessary raising of consciousness among those who have been taught that the ways of their ancestors were barbaric, pagan, and uncivilized. Second, tradition provides the critical constructive material upon which a community rebuilds itself.

Within this process, though, Deloria points out that tradition cannot be placed upon an idolatrous pedestal. Further, the changes that centuries of oppression have wrought upon those traditions must be taken into consideration in finding the wisest path toward a sovereign future. His comments during this time predicted the best of what has happened in many reservation communities since Wounded Knee. Though the antagonisms among different groups remain, community-based activists and leaders have moved toward bringing together tradition and pragmatic politics in such areas as substance abuse, tribal government, and education.

After Wounded Knee, the leaders of the American Indian Movement (AIM) spent most of their time in court or as fugitives. In Deloria's words, they "understand the gut issues that people of reservation communities and in the cities really care about. . . . They can rally a high percentage of people in any Indian community because they are really at the same place mentally and emotionally as those people are."[10]

At one level Deloria understood that AIM and other aggressive, militant groups had achieved mass support greater than that experienced by earlier national Indian organizations. At another level, though, he was concerned that the heat of the moment had guided Native activism into losing its sense of historical perspective and becoming a victim of its own success. With the movement "stalled in its own rhetoric" and no longer able to capture national attention, the conservatives and moderates on the national Indian scene found themselves reaping the greatest benefits of the often-courageous actions of AIM, other militant groups, and the traditionals.[11]

What the various movements were not overcoming, however, was the critical problem that much of what they did played into the expectations of the dominating society. As Deloria writes of the increased attention he and other authors were receiving, "Every book on modern Indian life [has been] promptly buried by a book on the 'real' Indians of yesteryear." He goes on to analogize as to what would have happened if African-Americans had received this same sort of debilitating exclusive fascination from non–African-Americans during their freedom struggle in the Civil Rights and Black Power movements. He has reporters asking Martin Luther King Jr. "about the days on the old plantation," deciding that he is a "troublemaker," and concluding "that everything will be all right if the blacks would simply continue to compose spirituals." He goes on to imagine the March on Washington being eclipsed by a new best-selling book, "*Bury My Heart at Jamestown*," that convinces white readers "to vow never again to buy and sell slaves."[12]

He further comments on the increasing popularity of Native American imagery in the environmental movement and in popular culture and on the growing number of books featuring words of wisdom from nineteenth-century Indians and sepia-toned photographs. Continuing his African-American analogy, he says, "Anthologies of spirituals become very popular, . . . sternly inform[ing] us we must come to understand the great contributions made by slaves to our contemporary culture. 'More than ever,' one commentary reads, 'the modern world needs the soothing strain of "Sweet Chariot" to assure us that all is well.' " Not only did these cultural dynamics that seem ridiculous in the African-American situation dominate the Native activist movement, Deloria asserts, but "a substantial portion of the public yearned for it to happen."[13]

Playing into these dynamics, according to Deloria, obscured deeper questions that the earlier generation had attempted to confront. These harsher criticisms come, for the most part, in less public, non-Native audience forums. "The deeper question," Deloria argues, "is really about how one becomes or remains an Indian in the twentieth century. A lot of the action is to return only to the external, show-business image of Indians, to wear feathers, long hair, dance and sing, and act mean all the time."[14] Thus, the pride and consciousness engendered by the militant actions was bought at a price. Calling Wounded Knee a "sorry melodrama" that was problematic because "it is clothed in the symbols of yesteryear," Deloria says:

> The widespread Indian failure to comprehend the experiences of the immediate past is matched by the inability of whites to relate to the modern Indian. . . . Whites look at the most profound and sacrificial efforts of contemporary Indians and find them wanting because they, the whites, can only relate to the Indians of the past they come to know through movies and television. Confrontation on the level of ideas becomes impossible, and misunderstanding abounds. Indians have won a temporary visibility with the media recognition of their problems. The price of that victory for all of us was the missed opportunity to understand the nature of the deep gulf separating Indian and non-Indian.[15]

Deloria's criticism here and in other places is not that direct action or even violence are intrinsically wrong, but that any political activism must bring with it critical reflection and constructive strategy.

He echoes this sentiment in another evaluation of the Native and other activism of the time that had "forever altered our lives" by saying, "The bitterness of reflection these days dwells not on what was accomplished but on what could have been accomplished had [people] been reasonable, just, or even consistent with themselves."[16] In perhaps his most fatalistic comment of the time, he says, "The most profound message we can manage is that history teaches nothing and [humans] learn little from generation to generation. . . . It would seem that Indians and whites were somehow destined to be each others' victims . . . and perhaps that is what we must ultimately live with."[17]

Deloria's consistent discussion of sovereignty as an open-ended process has not often been paralleled among contemporary American Indian intellectuals. His straightforward warning against making the rhetoric of sovereignty and tradition a final rather than a beginning step remains an important reminder to those who engage in community, federal, and other American Indian work. I will argue that Deloria's analysis extends to American Indian intellectuals as well. That is, I contend that it is now critical for American Indian intellectuals committed to sovereignty to realize that we too must struggle for sovereignty, *intellectual sovereignty*, and allow the definition and articulation of what that means to emerge as we critically reflect on that struggle.

If, as Deloria argues, tradition cannot and should not be a set of prescribed activities, but rather a set of processes, does it not make sense that our work and our lives as American Indian writers and thinkers should be a part of those processes? Though the events that prompt this discussion are, of course, foreign to what was happening in Mathews's time, I will now turn to his work and argue that his great legacy is that he practiced intellectual sovereignty and, like Deloria, gives tremendous insight into the direction in which our work can now proceed.

Mathews on the Virility of Tradition

Although Mathews was not a direct participant in Osage ceremonies, he did have great respect for those traditions. He donated money each year to those who kept the *in-losh-ka* drum in Pawhuska and is fondly remembered by some people as a supporter of the dance.[18] Watching the dances, tape-recording the songs, and conversing with old Osages were highlights of his year.

In spite of his interest in and respect for these traditions, he was resigned, at least in his early writings, to their disappearance— probably within his lifetime. He was, as previously indicated, quite wrong about their demise. He wrote in the 1940s that he believed he was watching the "cleaning-up activity of militant, devouring Christianity; the cleaning out of the machine gun nests of native religion" (84). Peyotism was for him the last stronghold of the older times, combining as it does elements of the old ways and of Christianity. He felt that when the older people who continued these traditions died, though, "the old paganism [would] pass" (84).

Mathews was perhaps surprised toward the end of his life that the Osage *in-losh-ka* continued and was growing stronger even as missionary Christianity was losing its appeal among many Osages and other Native groups. He justified his belief in the end of those traditions both by his biologically deterministic fatalism and by his discussions with the older Osages, who also feared for the end of their traditions. His resignation echoed what these elders were saying to him. With the social system of clans no longer around to support them, he saw no way to stop the process of decline.

Mathews's belief that traditions were disappearing is best illustrated in his lifelong efforts with the Osage Tribal Museum. The museum was, for him, a way of conserving a memory of who Osages had been in earlier days. His goal, in coaxing nine men and three women to sit for portraits, was to immortalize in paint the images of those who would have been remembered in oral tradition in those earlier days. He says, "My life in the blackjacks being naturally sympathetic to conservation, and [because of] my deep feeling for the flow of time, . . . I felt that conservation could be very well stretched to cover some oil portraits of the old men [and women]" (126).

The portrait sittings reveal the quiet dignity and resentment, expressed humorously, of the full-blood Osages. Several posed in the Oklahoma August heat dressed fully in traditional clothes. One man "sat for three hours squinting in the bright light of the dazzling day. Occasionally he fanned himself, but there were no stirrings or grimaces to indicate the terrible discomfort of so much clothing" (133). When the artist finished, the sitter said, "Come back to-molla; I paint you" (135).[19] Another of the portrait sitters said, "Tell this white man he must send his daughter to me. For this picture he must send his daughter—that is Osage way" (132).

Two of the three women who sat, Mathews records, "were detached and calm and punctual" (135). The third, though, "outdid the men in temperament" (135). She could not wait for the artist to finish before viewing his work. "Once," Mathews writes, "when she passed behind the artist as he worked, in the sudden housewifely busyness that expressed her unhappiness, she frowned at the back of his head and said to herself, 'O-skee-kah,' which means in Osage, among other things, liar and horse thief" (136).

When the portraits were complete, Mathews planned a celebration at the museum and the older people hosted a feast. His remarks about that event encapsulate his conservationist attitude toward tradition.

If we could have saved for posterity the picture of the descending sun shining through the strips of beef strung along the dry-ing poles; the women busy around the kettles; and the dancers of the four clans coming together for the first time in many years to dance to the earth rhythm of the drums like befeathered and gorgeously painted gods, then posterity would need to ask few questions. If we could have saved the picture for them of the old men who, though dressed, were too old to dance but sat with closed eyes around the dance ground in dream thought; or if we could have saved the picture of the dancers who, as they danced, saw nothing except that which was in their hearts, there would be little need to attempt to have their souls painted on canvas. (136)

Again, Mathews reaffirms his belief that he is observing the absolute end of the Osage religious traditions he had known as a young man.

This confidence that Christianity would totally replace these traditions seems strange because, like Deloria, Mathews saw the great beauty of Osage traditions as being their adaptability. Much of what Mathews describes, in fact, can still be seen in the *in-losh-ka*. Even more than Deloria, Mathews saw this adaptation as part of the biological process in which the rest of the landscape also participated. Further, Mathews believed that the Osage ceremonial traditions and social structures had not yet reached maturity when the pressures of European contact began eroding them. Rather, they were in the stage of virility.

Given this interpretation of the traditions, Mathews's confidence in the ensuing victory of Christianity triumphant seems inconsistent. As he says of life-forms that have their process toward maturity interrupted, they remain "intensely virile," waiting for the power of the mature form that blocks their progress to wane into senility. Mathews considered the virile days of the United States to have ended with the Great Depression, but he did not predict, of course, that just such a waning would occur in the dominating culture in the 1960s and 1970s and that American Indians would be able to continue aggressively the process toward maturity.

Mathews's process does give some insight into the experiences of the past twenty years for American Indian people. The events of that period, understood within his biological framework, provided the opportunity for American Indian people to move into the gaps of life force left open by a beleaguered power. In this way his work points in the same direction as Deloria's insofar as he suggests that the real challenge of such a moment would be to move toward maturity and a consolidation of a new area of the life force.

Mathews was perhaps impressed by the "virile" energy of the protests of the 1960s and 1970s, but he would have been even less pleased with the goals of the power movements than was Deloria. The terms self-determination and sovereignty connote in their most immediate sense much of the human arrogance that Mathews believed was the root of twentieth-century problems. They do not convey any sense of how limited human power and action are when they are part of, rather than against, biological processes.

The differences between the time when Mathews was writing and the watershed events of the 1970s are so marked that his work is limited in its ability to interpret critically the return to tradition and its meaning for an American Indian future. What Mathews does give tremendous insight into, though, is how American Indians can conceive of intellectual work as part of tradition and part of biological processes.

In *Talking to the Moon*, Mathews is obsessed with self-critical reflection on what he was doing in his life of writing at the Blackjacks. He presents a vision of how the act of writing functions in the struggle for self-determination and is continuous with both tradition and survival. Mathews's life at the Blackjacks, in this reading, becomes a long critical reflection on the meaning of freedom through the practice of intellectual sovereignty.

Both American Indian ceremonial traditions and the act of reflection and writing were, for Mathews, part of the biological processes of play, virility, maturity, and senility. As he grew toward maturity, observing life on the blackjack ridges and in Osage County and mulling it around in his mind was not enough. The demand to write was not for him a matter of pleasing the reading public but rather part of "the mature urge to ornamental expression" (14).

In and of itself, though, writing "couldn't satisfy me as an expression; there was too much that was inexpressible; . . . Physical action and living to the very brim each day in harmony with the life about me were exhausting and therefore completely satisfactory" (16). In other words, writing and reflection were not for Mathews activities that could be isolated from the material experiences upon which he was reflecting: "It seems that, in order to survive, [humans have] to follow the laws of the earth in all categories of [their] complex existence—[their] dreams notwithstanding" (3).

The beginning point of his reflection on both his own work and on the power of Osage tradition is the land itself and the processes through which it passes in adapting itself to new challenges. Using this approach (as argued in the previous chapter), he avoids slipping into a rhetoric that separates American Indians either from the rest of humanity or from their own past. He speaks in one place, for instance, of the way sitting quietly around a campfire with the Cow-wooly, one of his colorful rural white characters, is an activity continuous with the past: "With no medium of expression the depths of our souls remain unguessed and unappreciated, even by ourselves, even as the dawning soul of our ancestor, . . . gazing into the wonder of a fire, which sensed dreams that could only be expressed in fear and poignant emotion" (170).

The same fatalism that kept Mathews from hoping that American Indians could have some future in which the power of their traditions would once again be a possibility, also forced him to ask, "Why should I spend the golden hours attempting to express my thoughts and emotions in word symbols when I can't do so adequately?" (183). In answering this question he finds the red-tailed flicker singing its song "to a world busy with its own affairs," the "yapping of the coyote and the death chant of the Osage," and his own physical action much more satisfying expressions of his emotions (183).

For Mathews, this kind of satisfaction came mainly from hunting. He relates a story of hunting with Bill Whitman. Whitman, a white academic who was writing a monograph on the Osage, had never before hunted bobwhite quail, Mathews's favorite prey. After an exhilarating day, Whitman, scotch and soda in hand, exclaims, "You know, I feel like a god—a pagan one, of course; a rather tired one, but I have a superior feeling. . . . It's not right that men should be as gods; we must neutralize the mysterious glory that floods us" (183). Mathews answers, "That's the only way; . . . neutralize the glory—then eat steak and spaghetti" (183).

This leads Mathews to say that the danger of such a life—learning to live in the neglected power of natural processes—is its opening up of the possibilities of human arrogance and grandiosity.

Mathews, though, prefers a sense of humility that makes him feel like the character in Anatole France's "Our Lady's Juggler" who offers to a statue of Our Lady a display of juggling, having been told that the lady would accept the offering because "it was the only thing he could do, the thing he did best, and represented the limits of his ability" (183).[20] In this we find perhaps the most important statement of how Mathews thought of the work he did. He echoes Deloria's sentiment that intellectual work can make up one part of the social and political life in American Indian communities. Though some might criticize Mathews for being presumptuous in speaking of tradition while not being a participant, he evinces in his work a sense that such participation on his part would be inauthentic and would not represent his doing what he could do best.

Whether we regard Mathews's work as hopelessly romantic, overly bourgeois, virulently sexist, or wonderfully insightful, he provides an excellent starting point for envisioning an American Indian intellectual praxis that can help make sense of the spiritual, political, and social lives that we now live. Though he would not have used the terms praxis or sovereignty, his way of living at the Blackjacks and his ornamental expressions of that life are examples of how one person was able to bring together the various elements of existential struggle in a way that makes sense of the material realities faced by American Indian communities and the lands on which they live. Or at least his praxis leads him to the right sorts of questions.

Mathews gives us an example of intellectual sovereignty deeply committed to humanism. Only someone with a deep sense of humanism, after all, could write, "Often I ride to a point on the edge of the canyon just before sundown and sit listening to this indescribable song that seems to express all the yearning of the human spirit; the song that asks the eternal question 'Why?' so softly, so sadly, so submissively, as the day ends" (69).

As in Deloria's arguments about sovereignty, what operates in Mathews's coming "to the Blackjacks as a man who had pulled himself out of the roaring river of civilization" is a sense of withdrawal, critical reflection, and, perhaps most important, a focus on experience as the foundation of that work (3-4). This is more than simply removing oneself from the world and ignoring its presence:

One cannot appreciate what it means to step out of natural background where one has lived alone, with only the voices of the ridges, into the society of one's own kind. One being fresh and alert one's self sees only freshness and beauty in others. How beautiful are women in the soft light of the dinner table and on the dance floor, and how wonderful the music. How heavenly is the scotch-and-soda, the wine, and the taste of a cigarette, and how interesting . . . conversation . . . no matter what the topic. How clearly one seems to see the social, economic, and political problems through the spectrum of freshness, and how much greater is the magic of the indefinite "They" who have made the wonders of civilization; the magicians who have brought forth the radio, television, chrome-bright mechanisms, skyscrapers, and electrical gadgets. And how beautiful is romance, filling every cell of one's capacity for emotion, and how delightfully inspiring to ornamental expression. (125)

Mathews took seriously the situation in which he found himself and did what he could to resist the forces of death around him. His withdrawal to the Blackjacks, then, is the individual and intellectual equivalent of Deloria's analysis presented earlier. His voice of protest is not one that makes loud demands for recognition. Rather, Mathews finds for himself a place from which to give himself over to the process of moving toward the maturity of intellectual experience and action.

That withdrawal, importantly, is experience and leads to experience. For both figures, direct experience, whether of tradition or of the intellectual task, is central.

Religious Imagination in Deloria and Mathews

As discussed in chapter 2, Deloria's abiding criticism of modern Christianity is its concern for interpreting experience rather than having an experience. In modernity's concern for being able to verify through its own terms the experiences of the past, he argues further, religious scholars have assumed that what is really going on in tribal traditions is not based in actual events but in "childish wish predictions" and "superstitions that have arisen because of a great psychological need."[21]

Countering this haughty modern attitude toward tradition, Deloria says that we must begin discussion of tradition with a realization that the people with whom those traditions originated knew more about the specific places where they lived than Western science and Christian traditions can teach us. Their precise knowledge of planetary movements, the cycles of the seasons, and the behavior of animals reveals to Deloria not an attitude of childish fear but of an adult respectful openness to the world and a willingness to accept from the land what it offered.

What Deloria describes is again a process through which the people with whom these traditions originated were developing from their experience a way of life in which the knowledge they gained supported them and their future. Rather than trying to escape from the influences of the lands on which they lived through positing concepts such as individuality or eschatology, they remained in the world of experience. In doing so, he argues, they opened themselves up to powers that they could not see physically.

Mathews speaks of these forces as part of biology and ends up saying many of the same things as Deloria. For Mathews, the problem with Western culture was that it "cut the balloon of imagination from its earthly anchorage" (*Talking to the Moon*, 222). The brilliance of the Osage tradition, he argues, was the way Osages "feared the result of [their] own ornamental thinking and charged the wind, lightning, the tornado, the snake, the screech owl, and imbeciles with [their] own fear emotions" (222). This, importantly, is not the childish, primitive fear that Deloria counters, but the fear of a maturing people who recognize the danger their human agency represents. As Mathews says, "The things gave back to [them] the fear emotion with which [they] had charged them, as the earth gives back the life with which the elements charge it" (222).

What we learn from these traditions, according to both writers, is not that the traditions provide a set of actions that change us through mere performance of them. If this were the case, a great number of Boy Scouts, hobbyists, and followers of New Age religions would be radically different from what they are. Speaking of tradition in such functionalist terms, Deloria argues, requires us to "stay in a cultural ghetto and prey upon white guilt and ask [out-siders] to respect [Native] culture." With such a point of view, he argues, "all you are doing is preserving the exoticness of it, and every time you try to reach out you've got to use stereotypes to begin with and you crush the process of communication."[22]

If we learn anything from living in a culture dominated by the dictates of Christianity, then, it is that going through the motions of a religious tradition is often nothing more than going through the motions of a religious tradition. We say little about what possibilities traditions open up for finding a way to relate to the world of which we are a part. We do not make ourselves a part of a process of learn-ing from our experience. Most important, the focus of discussion remains on individuals and their consciousnesses rather than on communities and environments.

As any look around Indian country will show, the presence of tra-ditions does not in and of itself make the future. Rather, those tra-ditions make the future a possibility, just as they did for the people with whom the traditions originated. One way to become part of that same possibility is to follow the process-centered, experiential path of Mathews and Deloria.

We begin that process by opening ourselves up to experience and deriving from it the questions we must answer if we are to have a future. This is like Mathews's first year at the Blackjacks. Upon his return, as he tells it,

> I lived as part of the balance. There was no shouting and no firing of guns around the house. But a strange thing happened; I, under the influence of the following Planting Moon, broke the truce. I brought pheasants, chickens and guineas to the ridge. . . .
> Perhaps my position was unnatural, living as I did, not from the ridge, but feeding myself artificially from cans brought from town and food from the ranch. I was not a part of the economic struggle of the ridge which results in the balance, and therefore I was really an anomaly, as far as my own survival was concerned. After bringing pheasants, guineas, and chick-ens to the ridge, I had to fight for the survival of my charges against my predacious neighbors, which was probably a more natural state and in the end more satisfying than my "friends

and neighbor" idea. I became important to my predacious neighbors; the presence of my charges whetted their desires and sharpened their cunning. We learned more about each other; we found ourselves in struggle now and pitted our wits against each other and saw no more of each other in repose. We had greater mutual respect, and I became a part of the struggle through my strength to protect my flocks. Thus, I achieved a greater harmony with my environment and found there is no place for dreams in natural progression. (59-60)

We now face the same challenge intellectually in opening ourselves to the same kind of struggle. This is what Deloria seems to be saying when he portrays the challenge of the future as being one of posing the critical questions that arise when we undertake to reintegrate tradition into contemporary existence.

The process Mathews describes here is one of realizing that he was influenced by a great number of factors over which he had no control. What he struggled to do as he lived at the Blackjacks was to find a way of living as part of the balance that recognized these influences. He achieves what Deloria would describe years later as a "place-centered" philosophy. The same attitude comes through in all of his writing. In *Sundown* Mathews articulates a sense of how certain pressures were creating challenges for a community of people.

That history of struggle and influence goes back further than the late nineteenth century. Mathews's tribal history interweaves what was happening in seventeenth- and eighteenth-century Europe as part of Osage history and what was happening with the Osages as influencing European history. He deftly points out the ways in which the Osage fur trade and dominance of their portion of the trans-Mississippi West constituted a stumbling block for the broader aspirations of the French, Spanish, and English.[23] Far from surrounded, Osages, as Mathews saw it, participated in a complex network of international politics in which they had agency and influence. Mathews, because he was grounded in the experience of people, as well as the land that was a "character in the drama," and knew about the global history that influenced that experience, evinces a worldly interpretative scheme that has little room for simplistic tragedy and monolithic victims and victimizers.

This is not to say that Mathews had a complete understanding of those influences. Indeed, our contemporary situation demands a much broader range of factors than he included in his work. His view of females, for instance, blinded him to the power of the feminine in both the landscape and society. The important thing to point out here, though, is that the way Mathews writes allows the possibility for opening up the discourse. Both figures, because they refuse to rely on a single principle of interpretation, defy reductionist readings of their work.

The best example of this in Mathews comes from his tribal history. In *The Osages: Children of the Middle Waters*, he gives his reading of how the starting point for all tribal traditions after the Osages descended from the stars was confronting the disorder and chaos of the earth. Three major groups, as he interprets Osage oral traditions, came from the stars and encountered the Isolated Earth People, people living with "death, decay, disease, and waste, and the bones of [humans] along with the bones of animals" (14). Men were physically abusing women, and "might makes right" was the order of the day. This state, in the Osage language, is *ga-ni-tha*, and the joining of the groups represented the struggle of Osages to find ways of ordering their lives so as to prevent *ga-ni-tha* from being the status quo. They drew their lessons from the sky, which was more constant and predictable than the earth, and from *Wah'kon-tah*, the mystery force that they experienced (*The Osages*, 8ff.).

Not everyone in the community pondered the ways in which *ga-ni-tha* could be avoided. Rather, it was the *No'n-Ho'n-Shinka*, or the Little Old Men, who "moved . . . from the noise of the village and met each day during periods of tranquility under the shade of an elm" (*The Osages*, 21).[24] From their "inquisitive gropings" under the elm and later, in the Lodge of Mystery, they "created a formal religion, an organized buffalo hunt, an organized war movement, and a civil government" (21). "As the years, and even the centuries flowed on," Mathews writes,

> other men took the place of the Little Old Men almost each generation and added new thoughts to the fumblings toward an understanding of *Wah'Kon*, the Mystery Force, until there was a most intricate organization, including endless ceremoni-

als, songs of supplication, and very rich but baffling symbol-
ism. The generations of Little Old Men had been so impressed
by the orderliness of the sky that each new generation of them
became more and more hopelessly involved in labyrinthine rit-
ual in their attempts to bring earth's mysteries and whimsical-
ities, plus [humans'] frailties, into sky-order. (26)

In all of this, as Mathews portrays it, the goal was to understand
how humans could live in some semblance of social, political, and
spiritual order.

When the Little Old Men faced problems that they could not
understand based simply on observation and reflection, they would
send out young people to gather information for them (27). Simi-
larly, young people would scout out situations involved in hunting
and war. An example Mathews gives of this kind of activity is an
account of how the Little Old Men found the right substance to
smoke in their ceremonial pipe. Several messengers went out in
search of something smokable and brought back weeds and plants
that made the Little Old Men "grimace when they inhaled the
smoke" (73). Finally, one of the messengers brought back sumac.
The Little Old Men smoked it and said, "This is what we have been
looking for; the smoke of this brother [the sumac] shall represent the
prayers of all the people" (74).

As he interprets the past three centuries of "fumbling toward
God," Mathews points out that it was only when the influence of
the Little Old Men was undermined that the Osages fell into mis-
fortune. He argues that the creation of the Osage National Council
in the 1880s kept the influence of the Little Old Men in place in
spite of the U.S. Indian Agents' desire that the new form of government would replace that influence (720). As long as the traditional
form of group organization existed, Osages were determining for
themselves how they would face the future. The political battles of
the 1890s that resulted in the dissolution of the National Council
represent, then, the moment in which the people were no longer
recognized as having decision-making power over their own destiny.

Mathews, unfortunately, resigned himself to that projected state
of affairs and fatalistically accepted the U.S. government-imposed
form of tribal government. Yet he points out that the old form of

deliberation lives on, for instance in peyotism (753, 8). Thus, Osage fumbling toward God continues in spite of not being recognized by the U.S. government.

This traditional form of deliberation is an example of what Deloria is talking about in his recent series on education. He says, "old people, surveying a landscape, had such familiarity with the world that they could immediately see what was not in its place. . . . They went to work immediately to discover what this change meant."[25] He goes on to say that these people "eventually . . . recognized that the world had a moral being and that disruptions among human societies created disharmonies in the rest of the world."[26]

From this realization, he argues, came the clans and kinship systems, which "were built upon the idea that individuals owed each other certain kinds of behaviors and that if each individual performed his or her task properly, society as a whole would function."[27] Within this situation children and adults learned how to behave through the example of those who had piled up enough life experience to know something about how to relate to the world.

What emerges from this sort of life, Deloria contends, is a profound humanism, whereas U.S. education programs "do nothing for the whole human being."[28] Native educators need to return to traditional practices because, according to Deloria,

> A solid foundation in the old traditional ways enables the students to remember that life is not scientific, social scientific, mathematical, or even religious; life is a unity and the foundation for learning must be the unified experience of being a human being. That feeling can only come by remembering the early experiences of the Indian community as it seeks to establish the primacy of personality growth as the goal of life.[29]

He argues that without rebuilding into the educational process these community responsibilities, the struggle for self-determination will be a false one that encourages Euro-American values of professionalization, accumulation of wealth, and exploitation of land. In Deloria's words, "You can earn money but you cannot be happy or satisfied unless you first become yourself."[30]

In another context, Deloria suggests that to become ourselves requires that we "begin to probe deeper into [our] own past and view

[our] remembered history as a primordial covenant." Through such a process, he argues, Natives would "discern, out of the chaos of their shattered lives . . . a new interpretation of their religious tradition with a universal application."[31] This universal application would not result in principles or doctrines, however, but in examples to others of the necessity of authenticating human experience with the particular places humans inhabit. Mathews echoes this in *Talking to the Moon* when he says, "In order to survive, [humanity] has to follow the laws of the earth in all categories of . . . complex existence" (3).

The struggle for self-determination and sovereignty, then, is not an unrealistic attempt to live in the romantic old days, but seeks to live out a form of humanism in a new situation. Without rebuilding that radically humanistic tradition, though, we live in a false consciousness in which

> we are led to believe that we are prepared to exercise self-determination because we are . . . able to . . . compete with the non-Indian world for funds, resources, and rights. But we must ask ourselves, where is the self-determination? What is it that we as selves and communities are determining? . . . We are basically agreeing to model our lives, values, and experiences along non-Indian lines.[32]

Natives educated in the systems of the dominating culture, he says, must take control of their own minds and educations, and model to the rest of their communities that it can be done.

What Mathews's life at the Blackjacks suggests is that we can and should extend these articulations about sovereignty to ourselves and the work that we do. As suggested in chapters 1 and 2, American Indian critical praxis has often talked about tradition without experiencing it. What we need to do as intellectuals, on this reading, is to move toward our own definition of sovereignty that confronts the chaos of contemporary Indian lives.

When we consider what it is that intellectuals can do, we find, ideally, a life much like that of the Osage Little Old Men and their scouts—the withdrawal from the "noise of the village," as Mathews calls it, to reflect upon the critical questions that arise from life within the village. That kind of reflection, according to Mathews, requires freedom away from the day-to-day battles for survival that communities confront. Of course, sometimes that freedom is simply not possible. In those cases, as in times of battle or the buffalo hunt, the Little Old Men would perform practical tasks away from the Lodge of Mystery. The responsibility of that withdrawal, however, is to make the connections between what is going on in communities and the various factors of influence we encounter. Our subsequent accountability is, first and foremost, to those communities from which we come.

As we look at our communities and at our own praxis, we confront the existential realities of chaos, *ga-ni-tha*. We are not simply the bearers of the truth who will make everything all right. Elizabeth Cook-Lynn (Dakota) says of her work as a poet, novelist, and critic:

> The idea that poets can speak for others, the idea that we can speak for the dispossessed, the weak, the voiceless, is indeed one of the great burdens of contemporary American Indian poets today, for it is widely believed that we "speak for our tribes." The frank truth is that I don't know very many poets who say, "I speak for my people." It is not only unwise; it is probably impossible, and it is very surely arrogant, for *We Are Self-Appointed* and the self-appointedness of what we do indicates that the responsibility is ours and ours alone.[33]

The work of criticism in its various forms needs to follow in this same path and understand that we can give voice to the voiceless, but we cannot speak for them. Appointing ourselves as the vanguard of liberation or the bearers of truths unknown to our communities is, as Cook-Lynn says, at best an arrogant fantasy in which we "think we are more significant, more important than we are."[34]

The suggestion here, through analysis and example, is for American Indian scholars and writers to participate in the kind of engaged existential reflection that we see in these traditions of deliberation. We respect tradition, in this case, much as Mathews did at the Blackjacks—by confronting the chaos of contemporary life and asking where we have been and where we are going. The first question to ask in our contemporary context, then, is, What is the chaos we face? What are the "shattered lives" Deloria speaks of?

The primary responsibility we face in posing these questions is simply to speak about contemporary Indian lives and understand the ways in which, in the words of Simon Ortiz (Acoma Pueblo), "this America has been a burden" to us as human beings.[35] To embrace traditions without taking seriously the path over which we trod toward that embrace is to deny our own selves. In refusing to engage in that kind of denial, we confront both the power of our traditions and the painful stories of Native people who have suffered and continue to suffer, people whose ways of survival present us with the terrible beauty of resistance that rarely finds a voice in Native political processes.

With this open-ended perspective we can further humanize ourselves and our works by engaging our particular questions in the context of other Others around the world who face similar situations. Whether such engagement is fruitful is not so important as is opening ourselves, from the standpoint of intellectual sovereignty, to a wide range of perspectives. As in the case of the Osage messengers searching for the right plant to smoke in the ceremonial pipe, we may choose poorly and not find the right sorts of partners for engagement. But we will eventually find critical perspectives that are of great power.

The best illustration comes from Mathews. In expressing himself in word symbols (to use his term) and by going to the trouble of publishing those expressions, Mathews has invited all of us to be part of his life at the Blackjacks, to see and hear, however inadequately, those things that caused him to write as he did. He has included us among the people to whom he speaks as he speaks and listens to the life that surrounds and influences him and that he influences.

The task of criticism is to accept that invitation and to become part of the process by asking questions, challenging his interpretations, and allowing ourselves to find out whether the power on which he draws is available to us. We become his summer guests. Like good guests, we do not bother him as he stands cooking in "shorts and cowboy boots" in his little box kitchen. We appreciate the trouble to which he has gone in preparing food for us, whether it is bear, venison, duck, or spaghetti and eggs. We also enjoy the freedom of talking late into the night about the things that matter to us.

Our presence at the Blackjacks, of course, changes the conversation considerably, especially those July summer conversations that were dominated by the presence of white Europeans and Americans like Paul Sears. Sears may have been interested in conversing about Clements's climax theory of ecology, but our demands on the conversation could relate to the issues of inclusiveness discussed in chapter 1.

When we begin to bring these myriad Indian voices and Indian experiences to the Blackjacks, Mathews no longer seems like a Native American Thoreau. He is, rather, a person whose work becomes a living part of the ongoing struggle for a sovereign American Indian future. This Blackjacks discourse becomes more than the embrace of American Indian philosophy and traditions; it is also an embrace of people in pain and chaos.

We, as critics, can find within such a praxis a way of making ourselves vulnerable to the wide variety of pain, joy, oppression, celebration, and spiritual power of contemporary American Indian community existence, whether we find that variety in writing poetry, fiction, theology, or cultural criticism. Within that vulnerability we do not reduce intellectual production to mere aestheticism or functionalism, but find the sources of pain in explicit analysis of economic realities, gender differences, and a host of other areas.

To continue to illustrate intellectual sovereignty through Mathews's Blackjacks, we see that the process of sovereignty, whether in the political or in the intellectual sphere, is not a matter of removing ourselves and our communities from the influences of the world in which we live. In the various American Indian critiques of the society that dominates us, we find variations on the theme that Mathews laid down in *Talking to the Moon*—Western Christian culture and society is built upon the delusion that human beings as individuals and in social groupings can somehow overcome the influence of the nonhuman world and of decisions made by other humans.

If our minds, our consciousnesses, and our imaginations are in any way continuous with these same processes of influence, it matters a great deal what is influencing our intellect. Colonel Pratt certainly understood this when he carted young Natives off to Carlisle to "civilize" their minds. Pratt set up an either/or system in which his young students either accepted his overwhelming influence or ran away from the school and "returned to the blanket."

This educational strategy has not changed much since then except, perhaps, that it is now more subtle, more pervasive, and more local. As Mathews realized at the Blackjacks, we can do little to stop those influences from growing and finding new ways of asserting themselves in our lives. He also recognized, however, that he could, in his own small way, make choices to counter those influences. He further saw that the freedom he gained was not in and of itself enough to counter those influences. He could choose wisely or foolishly.

The intellectual process is just as open to influence, of course, and we see in both Deloria and Mathews how intellectual influences work in what they have written. In Mathews we see heavy doses of Darwinism, ecological theory, and the kind of balance-of-power politics that prevailed in his time. In Deloria, we find a long list of non-Native influences such as Alfred North Whitehead, Immanuel Velikovsky, Paul Feyerabend, and Marshall McLuhan.

To tease out from their work the ways in which it exhibits "Indianness" would, by and large, miss the point of their achievement. We would not only shut ourselves off from the insights they have made, but would fail to recognize that perhaps their greatest insight was that to believe we can live free from and untainted by the rest of the world is to unwittingly play a parochializing, monolithic Anglo-versus-Indian game, the rules of which have been set up for our failure. The momentary intoxication of playing those games is perhaps necessary if we are to spark our minds toward some goal, but to continue on that path denies both who we are and what situation we find ourselves in. While we cannot help but be influenced, we can make some choices as to which agencies will do the influencing. One example of how this works itself out is contemporary American Indian poetry.

American Indian Poetry and the Critical Imagination

In 1976, as the energies of American Indian activism were quickly waning, an interviewer asked Deloria what would need to be done to establish new relationships between American Indian people and the rest of the world. "My approach would be, I suppose," Deloria answered, "extremely weird. I would say get all the poets of each group together. . . . Poetry is one means of describing the human condition that transcends institutional concepts and definitions. We need poets and expressions of insights by artists more than we need alternative solutions or institutions."[36]

Though he has expressed some disdain at the number of people who have overnight become American Indian poets because of the popularity of Native poetry, Deloria has also been impressed with the ability of poets to achieve in the area of writing the political and religious goals confronted by American Indian communities.[37] In the practice of writing poetry, Deloria sees an "effort to grasp from the fantasy-land of the white [person's] mind, a sense of historical being. In the poetry of the modern American Indian we find a raging beyond nobility that calls for recognition of the humanity and nationality of Indian existence."[38]

The achievement of the poets, then, is bridging the gaps in American Indian existence, past, present, and future. In the great variety of American Indian poetry we see people who try to make sense of the various factors that influence their ability to express themselves. Poets are able to give voice to experience in a way that links these factors. "Our poets," Deloria writes, "are the only ones today who can provide this bridge, this reflective statement of what it means and has meant to live in a present which is continually overwhelmed by the fantasies of others of the meaning of past events."[39]

A good example of how poetic and other writing has opened American Indian discourse comes from a collection by Beth Brant (Mohawk), *A Gathering of Spirit*.[40] Along with established poets, Brant includes in the volume a number of Native women prisoners. We learn from these writers that the prisons that limit our existence are not as limiting as we might think. The great beauty of Brant's collection is the way it creates space for these sources of power to emerge. The contributors' notes give striking examples of how some American Indian writers react to that freedom. Alice Bowen (Navajo) comments, "I have never had my work taken seriously before now." "All you closet Indian feminists," Gayle Two Eagles (Lakota) writes, "come out!"[41] Within the space of creative writing, these women speak powerfully about the joys, sorrows, and oppressive situations of their lives and feel free to write about what it means to be an American Indian lesbian, to experience domestic violence, or to engage in political activism and community activism in situations where men often have little respect for and give no support to their work.

These writers are, in a sense, exercising the kind of intellectual sovereignty articulated in this chapter. Most of them are acutely aware of the influences (or lack thereof) on their lives from oral tradition, from the non-Native poets from whom they have learned, and from the particularity of their own experiences. Criticism, of course, is not and should not be poetry. What we need to learn from the poetry is that we do not have to wait to discover some essentially Indian form of writing before we can begin to try to make some critical sense of our past, present, and future.

Perhaps the greatest lesson of Indian poetry is that it has often shown us not only how tradition is able to live in new written forms, but that it does not have to dress up in beads and feathers in order to be powerful. As Deloria points out, "Only the poet in his [or her] frightful solitude and in his [or her] ability to transcend chronological existence can build that spiritual bridge which enables individuals to travel the roads of [human] experiences."[42] However much these writers are performing an activity somehow continuous with that of storytellers and singers, they are also doing what poetry has done in its European forms and in other non-European contexts.

To reduce Native poetry either to its European or Native influences does little to reconcile either important feature of contemporary poetry. We could not, for instance, ask as critics how it is that these poets have taken a European written form thousands of years old and transformed it so easily to become a form of resistance against other European forms and systems. Poetry has provided a vehicle for such resistance because of the way it can unsettle prevailing ideologies and give voice to what is not being spoken within a culture.

In developing American Indian critical studies, we need to practice the same sort of intellectual sovereignty that many Native poets practice. As many of the poets find their work continuous with, but not circumscribed by, Native traditions of storytelling or ceremonial chanting, we can find the work of criticism continuous with Native traditions of deliberation and decision making. Holding these various factors (sovereignty, tradition, community, process, and so on) in tension while attempting to understand the role of critics in an American Indian future is of crucial importance.

An intellectual and critical praxis in which we focus on such tensions, differences, and processes confronts us with the material reality American Indian people face in the struggle for self-determination. For if we are to build American Indian nations (or whatever other project of self-determination Indians engage in), experience tells us what problems we must confront and resources we will utilize in reaching our goals. In the concrete materiality of experience, we see both the dysfunctions colonization has created for Indian communities and the various ways Indian people have attempted to endure those dysfunctions. The intellectual work of critics in the self-determination process, as shown in Mathews and Deloria, is drawing out of this materiality what this means and has meant. Along with the resilient power of traditions, these issues are the central concerns of Deloria and Mathews.

To illustrate more specifically how we can use a framework of intellectual sovereignty to unlock the silenced voices of women and others, I will turn to the contributions by Jimmie Durham (Cherokee) and Wendy Rose (Hopi/Miwok) to *I Tell You Now*, a collection of autobiographical essays by Native writers. In doing so I am in effect inviting them to join in Mathews's Blackjacks discourse.

Durham, who founded the International Indian Treaty Council of the American Indian Movement in the 1970s, is also a poet and visual artist. His essay about the sources and reasons for his poetry is a strong critique of contemporary American Indian politics, including the movement in which he was active. In the conclusion of the original version of the essay, he says, "Charlene LaPointe just showed me that those battered Sioux women in that shelter she runs on the Rosebud Reservation are my sisters turning to face an old century, turning to face a new one."[43]

After showing the essay to friends, he decided to emend it. They made several criticisms, mostly involving style and his need of a more self-revealing aesthetic. He responds by saying that he writes not for peace, love, or understanding, but because he hates this country. "Not just the government," he says, "but the culture, the group of people called Americans. The country. I hate the country. I HATE AMERICA." The problem of contemporary Indian politics is that "so many Indians don't seem to . . . hate this country. . . . We hate ourselves and each other instead, and now there we all are, out there trying to impress the white folks with one thing or another."[44]

Durham goes on to argue that this self-hate manifests itself through

> our intelligentsia, the writers and artists, [who] are a bunch of stuck-up, apolitical, money-grubbing, and flaky rip-off artists, and our political leaders [who] are usually crooks and pretentious bastards or . . . somebody's puppets. Our regular folks are usually drunk or bad-mouthing their neighbors. Do you know that out on the res we have just as much child abuse and wife-beating as the rest of the country? Alienated, man; this is definitely not the old days. . . . Our elders are all off being gurus to some white weirdos and talking about how some big earthquake or flood is going to solve all of our problems.[45]

In the midst of a creative, autobiographical essay, Durham speaks strongly of the contradictions that Native artists face. This is especially true insofar as he links Indian political and social dysfunctions to self-hate, much as Mathews did in *Sundown*. To develop a full analysis of these topics would require reading across other texts to gain other perspectives, but Durham brings to the Blackjacks a starting point for much-needed discussions.

Perhaps the best example of how experience-based criticism of American Indian creative writing can open up important discussions is provided by Wendy Rose. Although Paula Gunn Allen and others have argued that Rose expresses an essential Indian consciousness, Rose's own description of her work clearly rejects this kind of essentialism.[46]

In an interview, Joseph Bruchac (Abenaki) asked Rose if she agreed with people who say her work seems to derive from Native oral traditions. Rose answered:

> I would like to but I would have to say probably not too much. I think there are some important differences, and I think my particular work probably leans more toward Euro-

pean-derived ideas of what poetry is and who poets are than Native American in spite of the subjective feeling I have of the way the poems are used in my life. There are some important differences, one of which is the sense of self-expression. The need to express the self, the need to make one's own emotions special and to explain it to other people, I don't think really exists in most Native American cultures. And I think that is an important component of my work.[47]

Rose reminded Bruchac of what he already knew well—that she grew up far from the traditional culture that supposedly is influencing her consciousness—but he returned to his essentialist themes several times in the interview. Each time, Rose responded by saying that the important thing about her work is how it functions in her life and in the lives of people who read and hear her poems.[48]

In her autobiographical essay in *I Tell You Now*, Rose is more direct in expressing the pain she feels when people posit these common experiences and essential consciousnesses for American Indian people. She describes the difficulty with which she wrote the essay:

Everything I have ever written is fundamentally autobiographical, no matter what the topic or style; to state my life now in an orderly way with clear language is actually to restate, simplified, what has already been said. If I could just come right out and state it like that, as a matter of fact, I would not have needed the poetry. If I could look my childhood in the eye and describe it, I would not have had to veil those memories in metaphor. If I had grown up with a comfortable identity, I would not need to explain myself from one or another persona.[49]

She goes on, in excruciating detail, to talk about how her mother's family, which has an embarrassing (to them) Miwok ancestor on its family tree, expressed their internalized racism through neglecting Rose and beating her until she had "bruises that rise on my flesh like blue marbles." Her stepfather also abused her, augmenting his beatings of her by naming "the parts of my body he intended to mutilate or cut away."[50]

Later in the essay, she asks, "How do you reconcile being an 'Indian writer' with such a non-Indian upbringing? It is not the Indian way to be left so alone, to be alienated, to be friendless."[51] Rose is exactly right. And anyone who is willing to listen to the voices in Indian country knows that Rose is not alone. In breaking her own silence, Rose brings to the Blackjacks conversation a stark reminder of the need for healing in Indian communities and presents a profound challenge for American Indian intellectuals to be more honest, more inclusive, and to recognize the profound challenges we face.

At the end of her essay Rose speaks of a visit to the Hopi father who abandoned her. He told her, "That Hopi earth does contain my roots and I am, indeed, from that land. Because the roots are there, I will find them. But when I find them," he said, "I must rebuild myself as a Hopi."[52]

In the interview with Bruchac, she talked about how she develops this idea in her poem "Builder Kachina."[53] In Hopi tradition, she comments in a note to the poem, there is no Builder Kachina: "The identities and roles of the Kachina Holy People are traditionally somewhat flexible; this is one that is not part of the Hopi tradition, but is part of my imagination."[54] Rose invents the Builder Kachina to respond to the need in her life to construct for herself an identity, not traditionally Hopi and not Euro-American, one in which she can find the roots her father spoke of. Her powerful poem ends as follows:

> Carefully
> the way we plant the corn
> in single places, each place
> a hole just one finger around.
> We'll build your roots
> that way. He said this
> as badgers marked their
> parallel lines on his skin,
> each one a clan mark,
> as Builder Kachina
> hooted beside him, invisible
> yet touching me all over
> with his sound.
> What we can't find
> we'll build but
> slowly,
> slowly.[55]

Bruchac, typically, turns discussion of the poem toward an imagined battle of European and Indian metaphysics. Rose quite obviously presents us with the material circumstances of colonization that require of American Indians creativity and adaptability.

To understand Rose is to accept in full both the particularity of her experience and her strong affirmation of Nativeness. From the experience that she and others have articulated so clearly and courageously, we can confront a set of issues that rarely appear in academic discourse—the vast numbers of Indian people who are invisible victims of racism, domestic violence, homophobia, and the process of colonization.

Along with these examples from Rose and Durham, we could also include in this discourse at the Blackjacks the large numbers of gay men and lesbians who have been cut off from tribal communities because of structures of colonial homophobia and compulsory heterosexuality. Allen, lesbian Indians, and gay male Indians have established the fact that, before contact, many Native groups did not discriminate against people because of their sexual orientation. Courageous articulations of their experience, through writing and activism, have begun to have an effect on Indian families and communities.[56]

Far from a discourse that is merely about the future of Indian sovereignty, this inclusive discussion itself becomes part of the future, a demonstration of possibilities. By withdrawing from the increasingly noisy village of discourse about Indians and embracing ourselves and each other in the fullness of our humanity, we can experience the fullness of our past, present, and future.

Exercising Intellectual Sovereignty

If we are to engage in intellectual work, we must critically reflect on both the limits and value of that work, as Mathews did. In his reflections he understood with great clarity how limited and unsatisfying were his own thoughts. He did not presume to come up with the key to life. He struggled daily to express through his body, on the ever-changing landscape, and among all living things, the joy that comes through struggle and resistance to power with his own power.

To follow his example we must in effect withdraw to the Blackjacks and engage in the same kind of reflection that Mathews did. If our struggle is anything, it is the struggle for sovereignty, and if sovereignty is anything, it is a way of life. That way of life is not a matter of defining a political ideology or having a detached discussion about the unifying structures and essences of American Indian traditions. It is a decision—a decision we make in our minds, in our hearts, and in our bodies—to be sovereign and to find out what that means in the process.

Such a praxis leads us into life in the face of death and teaches us that our knowledge can neither predict the future nor ossify the past. The value of our work then expresses itself in the constant struggle to understand what we can do rather than in telling people what they should do. As much as the revolutionary or the grassroots organizer, we are inserted into the life of a people, and our work grows from the same landscape as does theirs.

In this way we bring to that struggle abilities that may not be necessary, but which provide fire-fueling facilitation and analytic power to the building of a future. We can bring technical and critical knowledge of how the society that dominates us works. Through Euro-American-style education, we can bring critical knowledge of what has happened in the history of that dominating society that helps explain the situations in which we find ourselves.

In fact, perhaps our greatest contribution as intellectuals is understanding our experience in wider contexts. In comparing our histories and our contemporary lives with those of other American Indian people, we see the complexities of our various pasts and have an opportunity to learn how other people have confronted the same problems we face. More crucially, though, we begin to see the importance of choosing carefully whom we invite into the sovereign space that is our intellectual praxis.

Though we have been good at proclaiming our inclusion among the oppressed of the world, we have remained by and large caught in a death dance of dependence between, on the one hand, abandoning ourselves to the intellectual strategies and categories of white, European thought and, on the other hand, declaring that we need nothing outside of ourselves and our cultures in order to understand the world and our place in it. Mathews and Deloria, on this reading, clearly point out that such an either/or perspective is neither necessary nor possible.

When we remove ourselves from this dichotomy, much becomes possible. We see first that the struggle for sovereignty is not a struggle to be free from the influence of anything outside ourselves, but a process of asserting the power we possess as communities and individuals to make decisions that affect our lives.

We assert that same power and learn quite a lot when we engage oppositional discourse outside of Europe and Euro-America. As M. Annette Jaimes points out in her recent essay on American Indian women and feminism, such engagement can lead to solidarity and discussion of similarities of various struggles for justice.[57] Doing so within the framework of intellectual sovereignty allows us to enter the dialogue with both a pro-Indian awareness of our own strength and an openness to what the experiences of others have to teach us. We must, as Deloria suggests, withdraw without becoming separatists, being willing to reach out for the contradictions within our experience and open ourselves to the pain and the joy of others.

The decision to exercise intellectual sovereignty provides a crucial moment in the process from which resistance, hope, and, most of all, imagination issue. Such a perspective allows two things. First, it defines a perspective of humanism in which American Indian people and traditions are necessarily neither more nor less human than any others. However much we believe that Native traditions are more humanizing than the destructive ideologies and theologies of the West, that belief issues from how those Native traditions prove themselves to be a humanizing element in contemporary praxis and how that praxis is, finally, human.

Also, though, that humanizing perspective is situated within a context in which the humanity of American Indian people and traditions is rarely recognized or affirmed. In light of this we must take explicit steps to ground ourselves in the humanity of American Indian experiences of the world, expanding, as Deloria seems to suggest, the definition of the human and providing the ground upon which the truly humanizing work of criticism can happen. That work, at its best, attempts to intervene in particular processes and points toward a future that begins with our own decisions to take what control we can of our lives and experience the pain and beauty of living in this America.

When we do so, we can situate ourselves in the same place as those in American Indian communities who work every day not knowing whether what they are doing is going to have any lasting effect; in the same place as the earth itself, struggling to regenerate itself against the greatest odds anyone could ever have imagined; in the same place as Malcolm X, sitting in Alex Haley's car wondering in desperation how to live beyond the momentary power of counternarratives, saying, "They won't let me turn the corner"; in Alice Walker's mother's garden, knowing we have something to learn from it, but knowing we cannot until we put our sanitized hands deep into its soil and feel a power of resistance that remains there.[58]

We stand in the same place as Joy Harjo (Creek), thinking of a jail peopled with "mostly Black and Native men," listening to the story of one of those Natives who was shot at eight times outside a liquor store and somehow survived. In this poem that she dedicates to Audre Lorde, she says,

> Everyone laughed at the possibility of it,
> but also the truth. Because who would believe
> the fantastic and terrible story of all of our survival
> those who were never meant
>   to survive?[59]

This, finally, is the lesson we learn from Deloria and Mathews while sitting at the Blackjacks—realizing the fragile miracle of survival after five centuries of pain and endurance. That survival has come in spite of the limits of being human and the spirit of not being satisfied that those limits should keep us from at least saying something, even if only the moon will listen. As Mathews says:

> I am not satisfied to feel and enjoy the flood of emotion which earth and the mere fact of living inspires and continue to express the Force-rooted urge in action. I must now attempt to express the subtleties in word symbols, in fear that the people to come will not know that the great Ego has passed this way. I want them to know that I, too, have heard the thrush at twi-

light . . . that I have heard the coyote talk to the moon and watched the geese against a cold autumn sunset.

My egotism, born of the struggle, demands at this stage in my life, that I become an Our Lady's Juggler, with word symbols as my poor tool, to sweat at the feet of a beauty, an order, a perfection, a mystery far beyond my comprehension. (*Talking to the Moon*, 243-44)

Deloria offers a similar vision. In 1972, wondering if perhaps yet another final assault on the possibility of an American Indian future was about to issue from the White House, the halls of the U.S. Congress, and the U.S. Supreme Court, he writes, "Living cannot be postponed." The intellectual task, regardless of how overwhelming the situation appears, "must certainly involve a heady willingness to struggle for both long and short term goals and at times simply for the joy of getting one's nose bloodied while blackening the other guy's eye. [It] has nothing to do with jobs, divine callings, political platforms, or wisdom and knowledge of the world. It is the solitary acknowledgement that the question of [human] life and identity is to let the bastards know you've been there and that it is always a good day to die. We are therefore able to live."[60]

Standing before the world of beauty and terror in this way is the final goal of being human and of being alive. It is a way of saying, "I will live in spite of what is going on before my eyes, in spite of every prophet of doom and destruction." For whatever reason, we have survived and can live—in spite of the best efforts of many to ensure that we would not and often in spite of ourselves. Our struggle at the moment is to continue to survive and work toward a time when we can replace the need for being preoccupied with survival with a more responsible and peaceful way of living within communities and with the ever-changing landscape that will ever be our only home.

Notes

Introduction

1. Vine Deloria Jr., "Worshiping the Golden Calf: Freedom of Religion in Scalia's America," *New World Outlook* 52 (1, September-October 1991): 22-24.

2. John Joseph Mathews, *Talking to the Moon: Wildlife Adventures on the Plains and Prairies of Osage Country* (Norman: University of Oklahoma Press, 1945), 98.

3. For a review of recent complaints against academic criticism, see Daniel Littlefield Jr., "American Indians, American Scholars, and the American Literary Canon," *American Studies* 33 (Fall 1992): 95-111.

4. See, for instance, Ward Churchill, "White Studies: The Intellectual Imperialism of Contemporary U.S. Education," *Integrateducation* 19 (1-2, 1982): 51-57; and Churchill's essays collected in *Indians Are Us? Culture and Genocide in Native North America* (Monroe, Maine: Common Courage, 1994), and *Fantasies of the Master Race: Literature, Cinema, and the Colonization of American Indians*, ed. M. Annette Jaimes (Monroe, Maine: Common Courage, 1992). For Jaimes, see M. Annette Jaimes, "American Indian Studies: Toward an Indigenous Model," *American Indian Culture and Research Journal* 11 (3, 1987): 1-16. Jaimes, in that article, outlines other essentialist "indigenist" and "Fourth World" positions. For a critique of Churchill's and Jaimes's projects, see Roxanne Dunbar Ortiz, "The Fourth World and Indigenism: Politics of Isolation and Alternatives," *Journal of Ethnic Studies* 12 (1, Spring 1984): 79-105. Churchill, like Jimmie Durham and others cited in this work, has been under scrutiny as of late regarding whether or not he is an American Indian person. Since in many cases such scrutiny has been occasioned by a broader political agenda that seeks to discredit some of the most politically radical voices in American Indian discourse, I have retained the references and citations. Further, and perhaps most important, the figures included here have been a generally accepted part of the discourse of American Indian studies during the years in which the questions I ask were articulated.

5. Paula Gunn Allen, *The Sacred Hoop: Recovering the Feminine in American Indian Traditions* (Boston: Beacon, 1986), 165.

6. A good example is Rebecca Tsosie, "Surviving the War by Singing the Blues: The Contemporary Ethos of American Indian Political Poetry," *American Indian Culture and Research Journal* 10 (3, 1986): 25-51. In that essay Tsosie makes a powerful argument that has little need for an essentialized consciousness, but includes a long section on unitary indigenous worldviews.

7. Jack Forbes, "Colonialism and Native American Literature: Analysis," *Wicazo Sa Review* 3 (1987): 17-23; Jimmie Durham, "Those Dead Guys for a Hundred Years," in *I Tell You Now: Autobiographical Essays by Native American Writers*, ed. Brian Swann and Arnold Krupat (Lincoln: University of Nebraska Press, 1987), 155-65; and Jimmie Durham, "American Indian Culture: Traditionalism and Spiritualism in a Revolutionary Struggle," unpublished essay, n.d.

8. Kate Shanley, "Thoughts on Indian Feminism," in *A Gathering of Spirit: A Collection by North American Indian Women*, ed. Beth Brant (Mohawk) (Rockland, Maine: Sinister Wisdom, 1984), 213-15; Chrystos, "I Don't Understand Those Who Have Turned Away from Me" and "No Rock Scorns Me as Whore," in *This Bridge Called My Back: Writings by Radical Women of Color*, ed. Cherríe Moraga and Gloria Anzaldúa, 2d ed. (Watertown, Mass.: Persephone, 1981; (New York: Kitchen Table/Women of Color Press, 1983), 68-70, 243-45 (page citations are to the 2d edition); Barbara Cameron, "Gee, You Don't Seem like an Indian from the Reservation," in *This Bridge*, ed. Moraga and Anzaldúa, 46-52.

9. Kimberly M. Blaeser, "Learning 'The Language the Presidents Speak': Images and Issues of Literacy in American Indian Literature," *World Literature Today* 66 (2, Spring 1992): 230-35; Kimberly M. Blaeser, "Gerald Vizenor: Writing—In the Oral Tradition," Ph.D. dissertation, University of Notre Dame, 1990. (Norman: University of Oklahoma Press, forthcoming); Katherine Shanley, " 'Only an Indian': The Prose and Poetry of James Welch," forthcoming.

10. For a selection from Vizenor's vast oeuvre, see the Bibliography.

11. M. Annette Jaimes with Theresa Halsey, "American Indian Women at the Center of Indigenous Resistance in Contemporary Native America," in *The State of Native America: Genocide, Colonization, and Resistance*, ed. M. Annette Jaimes (Boston: South End, 1991), 311-44; Ward Churchill, "I Am Indigenist," in *Struggle for the Land: A Land Rights Reader* (Monroe, Maine: Common Courage, 1993), 403-51. Though Churchill retains some concern in "I Am Indigenist" with a unitary indigenous experience, he focuses much more on a definition of his ideology that relies on political practices rather than on consciousness.

12. Forbes, "Colonialism and Native American Literature," 20.

13. Greg Sarris, *Keeping Slug Woman Alive: A Holistic Approach to American Indian Texts* (Berkeley: University of California Press, 1993), esp. 180.

14. Vine Deloria Jr., *Custer Died for Your Sins: An American Indian Manifesto* (New York: Macmillan, 1969), 265.

15. A. A. Carr (Navajo), *Eye Killers* (Norman: University of Oklahoma Press, in press); Joy Harjo (Creek), *In Mad Love and War* (Middletown, Conn.: Wesleyan University Press, 1990), 21, 51; James Welch, *The Indian Lawyer* (New York: Norton, 1990).

16. For a general discussion of these writers, see A. LaVonne Brown Ruoff, *American Indian Literatures: An Introduction* (New York: Chelsea House, 1989).

1. Deloria and Mathews in the Context of American Indian Intellectual Traditions from 1890 to 1990

1. Russell Thornton, "Discussion," *American Indian Culture and Research Journal* 2 (1-2, 1978): 29.

2. This is not to say that this same problem of ahistoricism does not exist in these other discourses. However, within these other oppositional traditions the

project of recovering and interpreting earlier work has been going on for at least twenty years.

3. Defining for myself what kind of Native intellectuals would make up the cast of characters for this study has been a constant struggle. In focusing on the works of public figures who published for a wide Native and non-Native audience, I am not discounting the intellectual contributions of writers whose main audience is Native or whose work is not written. In general, I have employed a wide definition of intellectual work that includes any activity that involves the political decision-making and analytic process, whether the impulses of that process are academic, journalistic, or ceremonial.

4. For an impressive bibliographic example of how broadening the range of Native writing makes a larger pool of texts available, see "Books by Iroquois Authors (Mohawk, Seneca, Cayuga, Tuscarora, Oneida, and Onondaga)," *American Indian Quarterly* 6 (3-4, Fall-Winter 1982): 358-76.

5. For discussions, bibliographies, and sample work of these and other earlier writers, see Bernd Peyer, ed., *The Elders Wrote: An Anthology of Early Prose by North American Indians, 1768-1931* (Berlin: Dietrich Reimer Verlag, 1982); Bernd Peyer, ed., *The Singing Spirit: Early Short Stories by North American Indians* (Tucson: University of Arizona Press, 1989); Margot Liberty, ed., *American Indian Intellectuals: 1976 Proceedings of the American Ethnological Society* (St. Paul: West, 1978); A. LaVonne Brown Ruoff, *American Indian Literatures: An Introduction, Bibliographic Review, and Selected Bibliography* (New York: Modern Language Association, 1990); and A. LaVonne Brown Ruoff, "Justice for Indians and Women: The Protest Fiction of Alice Callahan and Pauline Johnson," *World Literature Today* 66 (2, Spring 1992): 249-55.

6. Charles A. Eastman (Ohiyesa), *From the Deep Woods to Civilization: Chapters in the Autobiography of an Indian* (Boston: Little, Brown, 1916, 1936; Lincoln: University of Nebraska Press, 1977), 76ff. See also David R. Miller, "Charles Alexander Eastman, the 'Winner': From Deep Woods to Civilization," in *American Indian Intellectuals*, ed. M. Liberty, 61.

7. Eastman, *Deep Woods*, 92ff. See also David Humphreys Miller, *Ghost Dance* (1959; Lincoln: University of Nebraska Press, 1985), 248, 123.

8. Eastman, *Deep Woods*, 110ff. See also D. H. Miller, *Ghost Dance*, 253.

9. Hazel Hertzberg, *The Search for an American Indian Identity: Modern Pan-Indian Movements* (Syracuse, N.Y.: Syracuse University Press, 1971), 36, 44, 50, 76-77.

10. William Willard, "A Report on a Colonial Study of an Indigenous Other," unpublished manuscript (1991), 10.

11. D. R. Miller, "Charles Eastman," 62; Willard, "Indigenous Other," 11ff.

12. John C. Ewers, "Richard Sanderville, Blackfoot Indian Interpreter," in *American Indian Intellectuals*, ed. M. Liberty, 117ff.

13. Peyer, *The Singing Spirit*, 43, 75-77.

14. Hertzberg, *American Indian Identity*, 69. I have relied on Hertzberg in this section mainly for direct quotations from Natives and for establishment of historical events. Hertzberg's text is the fullest treatment of SAI, but the period remains one for which much could and should be thoroughly revised.

15. Ibid., 164.

16. Not all students who attended these schools became apologists for the system. Many escaped or, upon graduation, put Anglo education behind them, re-

donned traditional clothes, and "returned to the blanket" (returned to traditional life) (ibid., 18).

17. Vine Deloria Jr., "Out of Chaos," *Parabola* 10 (2, May 1985): 20. For a brief comment from Deloria about the SAI specifically, see "Landlord to Welfare Client: The Decline of the Indian in National Consciousness," *Humboldt Journal of Social Relations* 10 (1, Fall-Winter 1982-83): 124.

18. William Willard, "The First Amendment, Anglo-Conformity, and American Indian Religious Freedom," *Wicazo Sa Review* 7 (1, Spring 1991): 26-30.

19. Willard, "Indigenous Other," 18.

20. Carlos Montezuma, "The Repression of the Indian," *Wassaja* 5 (March 12, 1921), 2.

21. See, among several other titles, Charles A. Eastman, *Indian Boyhood* (New York: McClure Phillips, 1902); Charles A. Eastman, *The Soul of the Indian: An Interpretation* (Boston, New York: Houghton Mifflin, 1911); Charles A. Eastman, *Old Indian Days* [1907], intro. A. LaVonne Brown Ruoff (Lincoln: University of Nebraska Press, 1991); and Eastman, *Deep Woods*. Raymond Wilson, *Ohiyesa: Charles Eastman, Santee Sioux* (Urbana: University of Illinois Press, 1983), includes a full range of Eastman's writings in his bibliography (199ff.).

22. For examples of these figures' fiction and nonfiction, see Zitkala-Sa (Gertrude Bonnin), *American Indian Stories* (1921; Lincoln: University of Nebraska Press, 1985) and *Old Indian Legends* (1901; Lincoln: University of Nebraska Press, 1985); Charles Eastman and Elaine Goodale Eastman, *Wigwam Evenings: Sioux Folk Tales Retold* (Boston: Little, Brown, 1909; Lincoln: University of Nebraska Press, 1990). Also see Peyer, *Singing Spirit*, for short stories by Angel DeCora (43-48), Gertrude Bonnin (75-94), and Charles Eastman (95-118).

23. William Willard, "Zitkala-Sa: A Woman Who Would Be Heard," *Wicazo Sa Review* 1 (1, Spring 1985): 16.

24. Paula Gunn Allen, introduction to *Spider Woman's Granddaughters: Traditional Tales and Contemporary Writing by Native American Women*, ed. Allen (Boston: South End, 1989), 14; M. Annette Jaimes with Theresa Halsey, "American Indian Women at the Center of Indigenous Resistance in Contemporary Native America," in *The State of Native America: Genocide, Colonization, and Resistance*, ed. Jaimes (Boston: South End, 1991), 326.

25. An example is Prucha's massive history of federal Indian policy, in which the SAI and its members receive hardly a mention.

26. Willard, "Anglo-Conformity," 25.

27. For a book-length treatment of Bonnin, see Deborah Sue Welch, "Zitkala-Sa: An American Indian Leader, 1876-1938," dissertation, University of Wyoming, 1985.

28. Willard, "Anglo-Conformity," 28-29, 39.

29. See Peter Iverson, *Carlos Montezuma and the Changing World of American Indians* (Albuquerque: University of New Mexico Press, 1982), 34-37.

30. I do not mean to suggest that the various works walk lockstep one with another. Indeed, rivalry and envy seem to be as important features of many of the works mentioned here as agreement.

31. Hertzberg, *American Indian Identity*, 135ff.

32. Ibid., 150, 178.

33. Native writers protested against Anglo injustice from the beginning of the extant written record, but before SAI no organized movement of any Native political position documented itself in writing.

The sources I have used for African-American intellectual history are, among other titles, Harold Cruse, *The Crisis of the Negro Intellectual: From Its Origins to the Present* (New York: Morrow, 1967); Cornel West, *Prophesy Deliverance: An Afro-American Revolutionary Christianity* (Philadelphia: Westminster, 1982); and James H. Cone, *Malcolm and Martin and America: A Dream or a Nightmare* (Maryknoll, N.Y.: Orbis, 1991).

34. See John Joseph Mathews, *The Osages: Children of the Middle Waters* (Norman: University of Oklahoma Press, 1961), 401; and R. David Edmunds, *The Shawnee Prophet* (Lincoln: University of Nebraska Press, 1982).

35. See my "Dances with Ghosts: Pain and Suffering on the Big Foot Trail," *Village Voice* (15 January 1991): 33-37, for one account of the Ghost Dance movement and the Wounded Knee Massacre.

36. The literature on peyote and the Native American Church is vast, but much of it is not helpful in understanding the political praxis or the theological importance of the movement. Hertzberg's analysis is an exception (*American Indian Identity*, 239-84), but the best recent work on peyote in its historical and contemporary expressions can be found in *Wicazo Sa Review* 7 (1, Spring 1991).

37. Francis Paul Prucha, *The Great Father: The United States Government and the American Indians* (Lincoln: University of Nebraska Press, 1984; abr. ed., Lincoln: University of Nebraska Press, 1986), 218 (page citation is to the abridged edition).

38. For discussions of Native journalism, see Gerald Vizenor, "Tribal Newspapers," in Gerald Vizenor, *Crossbloods: Bone Courts, Bingos, and Other Reports* (Minneapolis: University of Minnesota Press, 1990), 290-94; James E. Murphy and Sharon M. Murphy, *Let My People Know: American Indian Journalism* (Norman: University of Oklahoma Press, 1981); Daniel Littlefield Jr. and James Parins, comps., *American Indian and Alaska Native Newspapers and Periodicals, 1826-1924* (Westport, Conn.: Greenwood, 1984).

An excellent analysis of the body-hating cultural and Christian impulses behind this and other repressive policies can be found in Richard Drinnon, *Facing West: The Metaphysics of Indian-Hating and Empire Building* (Minneapolis: University of Minnesota Press, 1980).

39. Willard, "Indigenous Other," 29.

40. Hertzberg, *American Indian Identity*, 152, 135ff., 147.

41. Importantly, SAI's problem was not that it was not present in Indian country. Indeed, its knowledge of what was happening in Native communities is much more impressive than that of a great number of contemporary figures.

42. Hertzberg, *American Indian Identity*, 20, 215-17. SAI and the Red Men, I should add, had significant conflicts.

43. St. James appears under several names in the literature. Raymond Wilson refers to him as "an odd character who kept changing his name" (R. Wilson, *Ohiyesa*, 162).

44. Hertzberg, *American Indian Identity*, 158. W. E. B. Du Bois was an associate member of SAI but had little to do with the organization (Hertzberg, *American Indian Identity*, 83).

45. Ibid., 165.

46. Ibid., 178, 200-207.

47. Willard, "Indigenous Other," 19.

48. R. Wilson, *Ohiyesa*, 184ff. Ironically, Eastman and others connected to SAI abhorred certain kinds of dressing up for show and worked with great vigor to stop Natives from participating in entertainment events such as circuses and wild west shows, even as they themselves did similar work as "platform Indians" (Hertzberg, *American Indian Identity*, 25ff.; R. Wilson, *Ohiyesa*, 141).

49. D. R. Miller, "Charles Eastman," 68-70.

50. I will not be dealing in depth with the Indian Reorganization Act (IRA) that came out of this period. For a discussion of the IRA, see Vine Deloria Jr. and Clifford Lytle, *The Nations Within: The Past and Future of American Indian Sovereignty* (New York: Pantheon, 1984). The bibliography therein includes a good representation of assessments of Roosevelt's Indian New Deal. See also Jennings C. Wise, *The Red Man in New World Drama: A Politico-Legal Study with a Pageantry of American Indian History* (Washington, D.C.: W. F. Roberts, 1931; rev. and ed. and with an intro. by Vine Deloria Jr., New York: Macmillan, 1971) (page citations are to the revised edition). The last chapters of this text (pp. 357-402), originally published in 1931, were composed completely by Deloria and provide a provocative counterreading to many of his other writings from the same period.

51. Garrick Bailey, "John Joseph Mathews," in *American Indian Intellectuals*, ed. M. Liberty, 207.

52. Terry P. Wilson, *The Underground Reservation: Osage Oil* (Lincoln: University of Nebraska Press, 1985), 26. I should point out that these categories are not strictly biological, but political as well.

53. Ibid., 189ff.

54. Ibid., 12.

55. Mathews, *Osages*, 771; T. P. Wilson, *Underground Reservation*, 38.

56. Bailey, "John Joseph Mathews," 207.

57. Mathews, *Osages*, dedication page.

58. Bailey, "John Joseph Mathews," 206.

59. Mathews, *Osages*, viii, ix.

60. D'Arcy McNickle, *They Came Here First: The Epic of the American Indian* (Philadelphia: Lippincott, 1949), 220ff.

61. T. P. Wilson, *Underground Reservation*, 39, 42, 88ff. This is but one example of the U.S. government refusing to recognize the legitimacy of a tribally created national government.

62. Ibid., 97.

63. Mathews, *Osages*, 777-79. Other Oklahoma Natives also became wealthy, but as individuals rather than as groups, because they had allotted subsurface and surface ownership.

64. Bailey, "John Joseph Mathews," 207-8; Mathews, *Osages*, 740ff.

65. T. P. Wilson, *Underground Reservation*, 132.

66. Ibid., 138, 146-47.

67. Bailey, "John Joseph Mathews," 208; Terry P. Wilson, "Osage Oxonian: The Heritage of John Joseph Mathews," *Chronicles of Oklahoma* 59 (Fall 1981): 270.

68. Ibid., 271-72; Bailey, "John Joseph Mathews," 209-10.

69. Bailey, "John Joseph Mathews," 210.

70. T. P. Wilson, "Osage Oxonian," 272.

71. Willard, "Zitkala-Sa," 15.

72. Prucha, *The Great Father*, 274; Peyer, *The Singing Spirit*, 75.

73. Deloria and Lytle, *Nations Within*, 55ff.

74. Ibid., 154ff., 254ff.

75. Prucha, *The Great Father*, 324, 325.

76. Hertzberg, *American Indian Identity*, 208.

77. Unlike the SAI, however, the National Congress did not bring together writers.

78. Peyer, *The Singing Spirit*, 76.

79. Hertzberg, *American Indian Identity*, 213.

80. Ascertaining the degree to which any of these works was instrumental in the reform movement is difficult, as is assessing the success of Native political activists such as Bonnin. These figures remain obscure in the written history of the Indian Reorganization Act, even in Deloria's otherwise admirable critical reading of the history of the act and its consequences (Deloria and Lytle, *Nations Within*).

81. See Ruoff, *American Indian Literatures*, 71, 132, 141, and Peyer, *The Elders Wrote*, 152, for general discussions of Oskison.

82. See also Ben Yagoda, *Will Rogers: A Biography* (New York: Knopf, 1993); David Randolph Milsten, *The Cherokee Kid* (West Chicago, Ill.: Glenheath, 1987); Joseph H. Carter, *Never Met a Man I Didn't Like: The Life and Writings of Will Rogers* (New York: Avon, 1991); and Ruoff, *American Indian Literatures*, 68-69, 137.

83. Dorothy Parker, *Singing an Indian Song: A Biography of D'Arcy McNickle* (Lincoln: University of Nebraska Press, 1992), 24, 28ff.

84. For discussions of McNickle's life, work, and bibliography, see Parker, *D'Arcy McNickle*; D'Arcy McNickle, *The Hawk Is Hungry and Other Stories*, ed. and with an intro. by Birgit Hans (Tucson: University of Arizona Press, 1992), viii-xiii; Peyer, *The Singing Spirit*, 160.

85. Mourning Dove, *Cogewea: The Half-Blood* (1927; Lincoln: University of Nebraska Press, 1981).

86. Dexter Fisher, introduction to *Cogewea*, by Mourning Dove, v. See also Alice Poindexter Fisher, "The Transformation of Tradition: A Study of Zitkala-Sa (Bonnin) and Mourning Dove, Two Traditional Indian Writers," Ph.D. dissertation, City University of New York, 1979.

87. *Coyote Stories* was originally published in 1933. Reissued by Lincoln: University of Nebraska Press, 1991.

88. Mourning Dove, in fact, worked in collaboration with an Anglo man, Lucullus Virgil McWhorter, and his editing and emending of her text explain much of the novel's difficult style and language (see Dexter Fisher's introduction to *Cogewea*).

89. New York: Dodd, Mead, 1936; reprint Albuquerque: University of New Mexico Press, 1936, Parker, *D'Arcy McNickle*, 68.

90. T. P. Wilson, "Osage Oxonian," 275-76. Mathews's first Oklahoma work, though, was a series of short stories and prose sketches for the *Sooner Magazine* between 1929 and 1933 (T. P. Wilson, "Osage Oxonian," 272-73).

91. John Joseph Mathews, *Sundown* (New York: Longman, Green, 1934; Norman: University of Oklahoma Press, 1988).

92. T. P. Wilson, "Osage Oxonian," 282.

93. John Joseph Mathews, *Talking to the Moon: Wildlife Adventures on the Plains and Prairies of Osage Country* (Norman: University of Oklahoma Press, 1945), 194.

94. Bailey, "John Joseph Mathews," 205.

95. T. P. Wilson, "Osage Oxonian," 284, 287.

96. Ibid., 278, 279, 269.

97. Ibid., 280-81.

98. Mathews, *Talking to the Moon*, 85.

99. T. P. Wilson, "Osage Oxonian," 282.

100. For comments on Indian leadership and traditionalism during the period, see Vine Deloria Jr., "The New Deal and the Indian Reforms," in *The Red Man in the New World Drama: A Politico-Legal Study with a Pageantry of American Indian History*, by Jennings C. Wise, rev. and ed. and with an intro. by Vine Deloria Jr. (Washington, D.C.: W. F. Roberts, 1931; New York: Macmillan, 1971), 357ff. (page citations are to the revised edition). See also Thomas Biolsi, *Organizing the Lakota: The Political Economy of the New Deal on the Pine Ridge and Rosebud Reservations* (Tucson: University of Arizona Press, 1992).

101. Ella Cara Deloria, *Waterlily* (Lincoln: University of Nebraska Press, 1988). Ella Deloria's quite delightful and insightful *Speaking of Indians* (New York: Friendship Press, 1944; Vermillion: University of South Dakota Press, 1992) shares with Mathews's *Talking to the Moon* the curse of having been published during World War II. See also Ella Cara Deloria, *Dakota Texts* (1932; reprint, Vermillion: University of South Dakota Press, 1992).

102. For an account of the termination policy, see Donald Fixico, *Termination and Relocation: Federal Indian Policy, 1945-1960* (Albuquerque: University of New Mexico Press, 1986).

103. Deloria, "The Rise of Indian Organizations," in *Red Man*, 371.

104. Vine Deloria Jr., new preface to *Custer Died for Your Sins: An Indian Manifesto* (Norman: University of Oklahoma Press, 1988), ix.

105. T. P. Wilson, "Osage Oxonian," 287ff., 289-90; John Joseph Mathews, *Life and Death of an Oilman: The Career of E. W. Marland* (Norman: University of Oklahoma Press, 1951).

106. Vine Deloria Jr., *Indians of the Pacific Northwest: From the Coming of the White Man to the Present Day* (Garden City, N.Y.: Doubleday, 1977), 160ff., 164.

107. Hunter S. Thompson, "Marlon Brando and the Indian Fish-In," in Thompson, *The Great Shark Hunt: Gonzo Papers*, vol. 1 (New York: Summit, 1979), 444.

108. Parker, *D'Arcy McNickle*, 181ff.; Deloria, "The Rise of Indian Organizations," in Wise, *Red Man*, 401, 375.

109. Paul Chaat Smith, "American Indian Movement," *Encyclopedia of the American Left* (New York: Garland, 1990), 22-23; Stan Steiner, *The New Indians* (New York: Harper and Row, 1968), 53. The Tuscarora's successful halting in the late 1950s of a Niagara Falls hydroelectric project sponsored by Robert Moses and the New York Power Authority is a direct action that mitigates Thom's claim. So does the first invasion of Alcatraz Island, which was happening concurrently with the first fishing protests. Along with the continuous history of intellectual production that spans the period from the Indian New Deal to the 1960s, a history of Indian activism at the local and federal levels should occupy a place in understanding the context of the 1960s. In other words, however important the actions of NIYC and other groups and individuals of the period are, they were not created ex nihilo. Rather, the actions of the 1960s built upon and reacted to what had occurred before. For an account of the Tuscarora actions, see Edmund Wilson, *Apologies to the Iroquois* (New York: Knopf, 1959), 126-68; for an account of Alcatraz I, see Adam Fortunate Eagle, *Alcatraz, Alcatraz: The Indian Occupation of 1969-1971*

(Berkeley, Calif.: Heyday, 1992), 14-18. Deloria's strong statements on the generational nature of Indian affairs are most evident in the chapters he added to Wise, *Red Man*.

110. Steiner, *The New Indians*, 74ff.

111. P. C. Smith, "American Indian Movement."

112. My grandfather, also Robert Warrior, was one of those who did *not* return alive from World War II. He died in Normandy, France, in August 1944. For a personal discussion of American Indians in the U.S. Armed Forces, see my "Reflections from the War Zone," in *Collateral Damage: The New World Order at Home and Abroad*, ed. Cynthia Peters (Boston: South End, 1992), 299-304.

113. Deloria and Lytle, *Nations Within*, 192ff.

114. Steiner, *The New Indians*, 23ff., 26-27.

115. Steiner, *The New Indians*, 85.

116. Ibid., 69.

117. Clyde Warrior, editorial, *ABC: Americans before Columbus*, reprinted as an appendix in *The New Indians*, by Steiner, 307.

118. Vine Deloria Jr., letter to the author, July 5, 1990.

119. Clyde Warrior, editorial, in *The New Indians*, by Steiner, 307.

120. Clyde Warrior, "We Are Not Free," in *Red Power*, ed. Alvin Josephy (New York: McGraw-Hill, 1971; Lincoln: University of Nebraska Press, 1985), 75.

121. Steiner, *The New Indians*, 70.

122. Josephy, introduction to *Red Power*, ed. Josephy, 1-2.

123. "The Country Was a Lot Better Off When the Indians Were Running It," *New York Times Magazine*, March 8, 1970, reprinted in *Red Power*, ed. Josephy, 243-44.

124. Vine Deloria Jr., *Custer Died for Your Sins: An American Indian Manifesto* (New York: Macmillan, 1969), 271. The afterword (pp. 268-79), from which this quotation comes, does not appear in the subsequent paperback editions.

125. Vine Deloria Jr., letter to the author, June 22, 1991.

126. For details of Deloria's biography, I have relied on one narrative account of it that he wrote as part of a *New York Times Magazine* article of 1970, "The Country Was Better Off" (reprinted in *Red Power*, ed. Josephy); the afterword to *Custer Died for Your Sins* (1969), by Deloria; and scattered comments in his writings and in Steiner, *The New Indians*.

127. Deloria, "The Country Was Better Off," 237, 238.

128. Ibid., 238.

129. A good example of Manichaean reservation politics can be seen in my report of the 100th anniversary commemoration of the Wounded Knee Massacre, "Dances with Ghosts." The agency Lakotas were most concerned with the publicity and attention they could receive from the anniversary, whereas the more spiritual and ceremonial Big Foot Memorial Ride was almost entirely a creation of the Kyle-Medicine Root District traditional axis.

130. Deloria, "The Country Was Better Off," 241; Deloria, curriculum vitae, 1990.

131. Steiner, *The New Indians*, 85.

132. Vine Deloria Jr., "It Is a Good Day to Die," *Katallagete* 4 (2-3, Fall-Winter 1972): 63.

133. Ibid.

134. Deloria, "The Country Was Better Off," 241, 242.

135. Vine Deloria Jr., quoted in Steiner, *The New Indians*, x.

136. Deloria, "The Country Was Better Off," 245, 244.

137. Deloria, "Social Programs of the 60s," in Wise, *Red Man*, 384.

138. Jack Forbes, *Native Americans and Nixon: Presidential Politics and Minority Self-Determination, 1969-1972* (Los Angeles: University of California-American Indian Studies Center, 1981), 110.

139. Vine Deloria Jr., *The Indian Affair* (New York: Friendship, 1974), 7-8.

140. See Cone, *Malcolm and Martin and America*, 19-57.

141. P. C. Smith, "American Indian Movement," 22-23.

142. Ibid.; Roxanne Dunbar Ortiz, foreword to *Native Americans and Nixon*, by Forbes, 4.

143. Vine Deloria Jr., ed., *Of Utmost Good Faith* (New York: Straight Arrow, 1971); *God Is Red* (New York: Grosset and Dunlap, 1973); *Behind the Trail of Broken Treaties: An Indian Declaration of Independence* (New York: Delacorte, 1974); *The Indian Affair* (New York: Friendship, 1974); *We Talk, You Listen: New Tribes, New Turf* (New York: Macmillan, 1970). The eight titles listed in the text represent Deloria's works that most directly engage specific events as they were happening in the 1960s and 1970s. Later books are listed in full in the Bibliography.

144. Deloria, "Conclusion," in Wise, *Red Man*, 401.

145. N. Scott Momaday, *House Made of Dawn* (New York: Harper and Row, 1968). Several other American Indians published during the decade before and after *House Made of Dawn* but did not achieve anything near the phenomenal success of the Pulitzer Prize-winning novel. They include Jack Forbes, ed., *The Indian in America's Past* (Englewood Cliffs, N.J.: Prentice-Hall, 1964); Gerald Vizenor's early volumes of haiku, *Seventeen Chirps: Haiku in English* (Minneapolis: Nodin, 1964), and *Empty Swings: Haiku in English* (Minneapolis: Nodin, 1967); Gerald Vizenor, ed., *Summer in the Spring: Lyric Poems of the Ojibway* (Minneapolis: Nodin, 1965) (recently reissued as *Summer in the Spring: Anishinaabe Lyric Poems and Stories* [Norman: University of Oklahoma Press, 1993]); Gerald Vizenor, ed., *The Everlasting Sky: New Voices from the People Named the Chippewa* (New York: Macmillan, 1972); Dallas Chief Eagle, *Winter Count* (Colorado Springs, Colo.: Denton-Berkeland, 1967); Frank LaPointe's *The Sioux Today* (New York: Crowell-Collier, 1972). D'Arcy McNickle, *Indian Man: A Life of Oliver La Farge* (Bloomington: Indiana University Press, 1971). Also worth mention here are Leslie Fiedler, *The Return of the Vanishing American* (New York: Stein and Day, 1969); Marion Gridley, *Contemporary American Indian Leaders* (New York: Dodd, Mead, 1972); Council on Interracial Books for Children, ed., *Chronicles of American Indian Protest* (Greenwich, Conn.: Fawcett, 1971); and Earl Shorris, *The Death of the Great Spirit: An Elegy for the American Indian* (New York: Simon and Schuster, 1971). Edmund Wilson's *Apologies to the Iroquois*, of course, preceded many of these works by nearly a decade.

146. Dee Brown, *Bury My Heart at Wounded Knee: An Indian History of the American West* (New York: Holt, Rinehart, Winston, 1970).

147. Deloria, *God Is Red*, 40, 41.

148. Forbes, *Native Americans and Nixon*, 75.

149. The Twenty Points document is reprinted in Deloria, *God Is Red*, 325-364.

150. Forbes, *Native Americans and Nixon*, 76.

151. I have based these comments on several published and many oral sources. See Deloria, *God Is Red*, 3-6; Deloria, *Behind the Trail*, 45-62; Forbes, *Native Americans and Nixon*, 75-102; D'Arcy McNickle, *Native American Tribalism: Indian Sur-*

vival and Renewals (New York: Oxford University Press, 1973), i-xxii; and Prucha, *The Great Father*, 366-67.

152. Ward Churchill and Jim Vander Wall, *Agents of Repression: The FBI's Secret War against the Black Panther Party and the American Indian Movement* (Boston: South End, 1988), 124.

153. Forbes, *Native Americans and Nixon*, 105, 107-10.

154. Gerald Vizenor, "Speaking for Mother Earth," in *Crossbloods*, 193-96.

155. Details about Wounded Knee come from sources already cited and from information gathered from oral sources; see Paul Chaat Smith and Robert Allen Warrior, *Like a Hurricane: How Wounded Knee II Changed Indian America* (New York: New Press, in press).

156. Deloria, *Behind the Trail*, 80. The resurgence in Indian pride, of course, had been a major category in the time leading up to Wounded Knee. The occupation did not initiate the affirmation of Indianness; rather, it increased awareness of an already-strong phenomenon.

157. Forbes, *Native Americans and Nixon*, 108.

158. Ibid.

159. Vine Deloria Jr., "The Indian Movement: Out of a Wounded Past," *Ramparts* 13 (March 1975): 30.

160. Vine Deloria Jr., interview with the author, Tucson, Ariz., August 5, 1989.

161. Willard, "Indigenous Other," 1ff.

162. N. Scott Momaday, *The Way to Rainy Mountain* (Albuquerque: University of New Mexico Press, 1969). Anyone who doubts the political nature of seemingly harmless creative writing needs to look at the travails of Momaday when he published his first work. It was picked over by anthropologists who said it was of no value in understanding American Indian cultures and by editors who subjected the work to social scientific, rather than literary, scrutiny. See Kenneth Lincoln, "From Tai-Me to Rainy Mountain: The Makings of American Indian Literature," *American Indian Quarterly* 10 (2, Spring 1986): 101-17.

163. Among these novels are James Welch, *Winter in the Blood* (New York: Viking, 1974); James Welch, *The Death of Jim Loney* (New York: Viking, 1979); Leslie Marmon Silko, *Ceremony* (New York: Viking, 1976); Leslie Marmon Silko, *Almanac of the Dead* (New York: Simon and Schuster, 1991); Gerald Vizenor, *Darkness in Saint Louis Bearheart* (1978), reprinted as *Bearheart: The Heirship Chronicles* (Minneapolis: University of Minnesota Press, 1990); Vizenor, *Griever: An American Monkey King in China* (Minneapolis: University of Minnesota Press, 1987); Gerald Vizenor, *The Heirs of Columbus* (Hanover, N.H.: University Press of New England, 1991); and Louise Erdrich, *Love Medicine* (New York: Holt, Rinehart, Winston, 1984); Louise Erdrich, *The Beet Queen* (New York: Henry Holt, 1986); Louise Erdrich, *Tracks* (New York: Henry Holt, 1988); and Louise Erdrich, *The Bingo Palace* (New York: HarperCollins, 1994).

164. The best example is Beth Brant, ed., *A Gathering of Spirit: A Collection by North American Indian Women* (Rockland, Maine: Sinister Wisdom, 1984). Brant's collection includes the widest range of American Indian women writers of any of the anthologies. She includes many Indian women in prison, middle-class urban women, and lesbians from reservations and urban areas, as well as many of the more accomplished poets. See also, among hundreds of examples, Joy Harjo, *In Mad Love and War* (Middletown, Conn.: Wesleyan University Press, 1990); Wendy Rose, *Bone Dance: New and Selected Poems, 1965-1993* (Tucson: University of Arizona Press, 1994); Sherman Alexie, *The Business of Fancydancing* (Brooklyn: Hanging

Loose, 1992); Maurice Kenny, *Between Two Rivers: Selected Poems, 1956-1984* (Freedonia, N.Y.: White Pine, 1984); Simon Ortiz, *Woven Stone* (Tucson: University of Arizona Press, 1992); Jim Barnes, *The American Book of the Dead* (Urbana: University of Illinois Press, 1982); Carter Revard, *Ponca War Dancers* (Norman: Point Riders, 1980); Lucy Tapahanso, *A Breeze Swept Through* (Los Angeles: West End, 1987); Ray A. Young Bear, *The Invisible Musician: Poems* (Duluth, Minn.: Holy Cow! 1990), and Chrystos, *Not Vanishing* (Vancouver, B.C.: Press Gang, 1988). For a broad range of contemporary American Indian poets, see Duane Niatum, ed., *Harper's Anthology of 20th Century Native American Poetry* (New York: Harper and Row, 1988); and Joseph Bruchac III, ed., *Songs from This Earth on Turtle's Back: Contemporary American Indian Poetry* (Greenfield Center, N.Y.: Greenfield Review, 1983).

165. Some examples of how American Indian writers have attempted to place unifying frames around Native discourse are Jack Forbes, "Colonialism and Native American Literature: Analysis," *Wicazo Sa Review* 3 (1987): 17-23; M. Annette Jaimes, "American Indian Studies: Toward an Indigenous Model," *American Indian Culture and Research Journal* 11 (3, 1987): 1-16; Paula Gunn Allen, *The Sacred Hoop: Recovering the Feminine in American Indian Traditions* (Boston: Beacon, 1986); and Allen, ed., *Spider Woman's Granddaughters*, 8. The strongest critic of these strategies has been Gerald Vizenor. Among many examples in his work, see the preface to his edited *Narrative Chance: Postmodern Discourse on Native American Indian Literatures* (Albuquerque: University of New Mexico Press, 1989), x; and Gerald Vizenor, *Manifest Manners: Postindian Warriors of Survivance* (Hanover, N.H.: University Press of New England, 1994). For other recent essays that wrestle admirably with the marked differences in perspectives on American Indian studies and Native intellectual work, see Elizabeth Cook-Lynn, "The Radical Conscience in American Indian Studies," *Wicazo Sa Review* 7 (1, Fall 1991): 1-8; and William Willard and Mary Kay Downing, "American Indian Studies and Inter-Cultural Education," *Wicazo Sa Review* 7 (1, Fall 1991): 9-13.

166. I have borrowed the descriptor from Annette Jaimes as a way to distinguish in an admittedly vague way between those scholars who associate and affiliate with radical politics and those who do not.

2. The Violation of Sovereign Land and Community in Deloria and Mathews

1. John Joseph Mathews, *Sundown* (New York: Longman, Green, 1934; Norman: University of Oklahoma Press, 1988), 4. Further citations will be made parenthetically in the text.

2. Louis Owens, *Other Destinies: Understanding the American Indian Novel* (Norman: University of Oklahoma Press, 1992), 49. Owens's analysis of the novel is the most complete to date. See it for a fuller, quite impressive summary of plot, tropes, and characters.

3. Though Mathews almost certainly did not intend it to be so, I cannot help but point out the irony of the phrase "stick it out" in the midst of the paddling incident.

4. Mathews's description of that decline is remarkably accurate in clinical detail, given the time in which it was written. For instance, he writes of the moment when Chal woke up after a party and "for the first time . . . he wanted more whiskey. He felt that he must have a drink. Every nerve in his body called for alcohol, and his head was bursting" (*Sundown*, 251).

5. Terry P. Wilson, "Women of the Osage: A Century of Change, 1874-1982," in *Women in Oklahoma: A Century of Change*, ed. Melvina K. Thurman (Oklahoma City: Oklahoma Historical Society, 1982), esp. 92.

6. Charles R. Larson, *American Indian Fiction* (Albuquerque: University of New Mexico Press, 1978), 15.

7. Ibid., 61, 36, 37.

8. Andrew Wiget, *Native American Literature* (Boston: Twayne, 1985), 77.

9. Carol Hunter, "The Historical Context in John Joseph Mathews' *Sundown*," *MELUS* 9 (Spring 1982): 61-72; and Carol Hunter, "The Protagonist as a Mixed-Blood in John Joseph Mathews' Novel: *Sundown*," *American Indian Quarterly* 6 (3-4, Fall-Winter 1982): 319-36.

10. Hunter, "Historical Context," 71, 335.

11. Owens, *Other Destinies*, 60.

12. Larson, *American Indian Fiction*, 78; Wiget, *Native American Literature*, 77, 80.

13. Owens discusses the changes *The Surrounded* went through from the time McNickle first submitted it to the publisher under the name of *The Hungry Generations* (Owens, *Other Destinies*, 62).

14. See Dorothy S. Parker, *Singing an Indian Song: A Biography of D'Arcy McNickle* (Lincoln: University of Nebraska Press, 1992), 29ff., for an account of McNickle's New York period.

15. John Joseph Mathews, *Talking to the Moon: Wildlife Adventures on the Plains and Prairies of Osage Country* (Norman: University of Oklahoma Press, 1945), 14. Mathews does speak directly in *Talking to the Moon* about his Los Angeles divorce.

16. See, for instance, Mathews, *Talking to the Moon,* 132. Further citations will be made parenthetically in the text.

17. An exception is A. LaVonne Brown Ruoff, "John Joseph Mathews's *Talking to the Moon*: Literary and Osage Contexts," in *Multicultural Autobiography: American Lives*, ed. James Robert Payne (Knoxville: University of Tennessee Press, 1992), 1-31.

18. For a fine analysis of the environmental history of this period on the plains, see Donald Worster, *Dust Bowl: The Southern Plains in the 1930s* (Oxford: Oxford University Press, 1979). (In subsequent quotations from critical sources, I have made changes to gendered language in brackets.)

19. Donald Worster, *Nature's Economy: A History of Ecological Ideas* (Cambridge: Cambridge University Press, 1977), 23.

20. For a review of Clements's theories, see Worster, *Nature's Economy.*

21. N. Scott Momaday, "The Man Made of Words," reprinted in *The Remembered Earth: An Anthology of Contemporary Native American Literature*, ed. Geary Hobson (Albuquerque: Red Earth, 1979), 164.

22. See, among many, Mathews, *Talking to the Moon*, 5.

23. Vine Deloria Jr., "Custer Died for Your Sins," *Playboy* 16 (8, August 1969): 131-2+.

24. Deloria has revised and expanded the book, adding material and updating many sections but making few significant alterations in the original argument (*God Is Red: A Native View of Religion*, 2d ed. [Golden, Colo.: North American Press, 1992]). All references herein are to the original edition. Further citations will be made parenthetically in the text.

25. Wiget, *Native American Literature*, 120.

26. This is true, for example, of Rosemary Radford Reuther in her *Sexism and God-Talk: Toward a Feminist Theology* (Boston: Beacon, 1983), 250-52.

27. Deloria's position on how Western culture and Christianity cannot be understood apart from one another has remained consistent since the mid-1970s. See Vine Deloria Jr., "Completing the Theological Circle: Civil Religion in America," *Religious Education* 71 (3, 1976): 278-87; and Vine Deloria Jr., "American Indians and the Moral Community," *Church and Society* 3 (September-October 1988): 27-38.

28. Though he does not discuss then-emergent theologies of liberation in *God Is Red*, Deloria uses the same logic in other essays in his critique of various non-European theologies that have emerged in the past two decades. For examples of Deloria's dialogue with Christian liberation theology, see Vine Deloria Jr., "A Native American Perspective on Liberation," *Occasional Bulletin of Missionary Research* 1 (3, July 1977): 15-17; and Vine Deloria Jr., "Vision and Community: A Native American Voice," in *Yearning to Breathe Free: Liberation Theologies in the United States*, ed. Mar Peter-Raoul et al. (Maryknoll, N.Y.: Orbis, 1990), 72-79.

29. Deloria, "Completing the Theological Circle," 279.

30. James R. McGraw, "God Is Also Red: An Interview with Vine Deloria, Jr.," *Christianity and Crisis* 35 (September 15, 1975): 202.

31. McGraw, "God Is Also Red," 203.

32. Ibid., 203ff.

33. Vine Deloria Jr., "Civilization and Isolation," *North American Review* 263 (2, Summer 1978): 13.

34. Ibid.

35. Vine Deloria Jr., "Perceptions and Maturity: Reflections on Paul Feyerabend's Point of View," in *Beyond Reason: Essays on the Philosophy of Paul Feyerabend*, ed. Gonzalo Munevar (Dordrecht; Boston: Kluwer Academic, 1991), 389-401, 394-95, 399.

36. Deloria, "Perceptions and Maturity," 391.

37. Vine Deloria Jr., letter to the author, June 22, 1991.

38. See Hunter, "Historical Context."

39. Vine Deloria Jr., "Religion and Revolution among American Indians," *Worldview* 17 (1, January 1974): 15.

40. Deloria, "Religion and Revolution," 15.

3. Intellectual Sovereignty and the Struggle for an American Indian Future

1. Vine Deloria Jr., *Custer Died for Your Sins: An American Indian Manifesto* (New York: Macmillan, 1969), 268-69.

2. Ibid., 267-68.

3. Ibid., 252ff.

4. Gerald Vizenor has been the most ardent critic of AIM. A good sample of his analysis of the movement is in Gerald Vizenor, *Crossbloods: Bone Courts, Bingo, and Other Reports* (Minneapolis: University of Minnesota Press, 1990), 157-96. Vizenor's criticisms were and are shared by large numbers of people at the local level.

5. Deloria, *We Talk, You Listen: New Tribes, New Turf* (New York: Macmillan, 1971), 114-37. For others, see subsequent references. Further citations will be made parenthetically in the text.

6. Michael McKale, "From Reservation to Global Society: American Culture, Liberation, and the Native American: An Interview with Vine Deloria, Jr.," *Radical Religion* 2 (4, 1976): 50.

7. Deloria, "Religion and Revolution among American Indians," *Worldview* 17 (1, January 1974): 14.

8. Ibid., 15.

9. Ibid.

10. McKale, "Interview," 52.

11. Deloria, "Religion and Revolution," 30; Forbes, *Native Americans and Nixon: Presidential Politics and Minority Self-Determination, 1969-1972* (Los Angeles: University of California-American Indian Studies Center, 1981), 124.

12. Deloria, *God Is Red* (New York: Grosset and Dunlap, 1973), 44, 46-49.

13. Ibid., 48, 49.

14. McKale, "Interview," 50.

15. Deloria, "Religion and Revolution," 13-14.

16. Vine Deloria Jr., "Non-Violence in American Society," *Katallagete* 5 (2, Winter 1974): 4.

17. Vine Deloria Jr., "Indian Affairs 1973: Hebrews 13:8," *North American Review* (Winter 1973): 112.

18. John Joseph Mathews, *Talking to the Moon: Wildlife Adventures on the Plains and Prairies of Osage Country* (Norman: University of Oklahoma Press, 1945), 79. Further citations will be made parenthetically in the text.

19. Mathews, much like Zora Neale Hurston, recorded dialect with great accuracy. Though this is not always true of his early work, he consistently translates Osages speaking in the Osage language in clear, grammatically correct prose. He also records Oklahoma European-American dialects very accurately. In doing so, it seems as if Mathews implies that native Osage speakers have an excuse for not speaking English well, because they are learning it in the midst of people for whom English is a first language, yet who speak it less than eloquently.

20. See Anatole France, "Our Lady's Juggler," in *Golden Tales of Anatole France*, by Anatole France (New York: Dodd, Mead, 1927), 102-13.

21. Deloria, *God Is Red*, 157.

22. James R. McGraw, "God Is Also Red: An Interview with Vine Deloria, Jr.," *Christianity and Crisis* 35 (September 15, 1975): 204.

23. For example, John Joseph Mathews, *The Osages: Children of the Middle Waters* (Norman: University of Oklahoma Press, 1961), 135ff. Subsequent citations will be made parenthetically in the text.

24. Mathews comments that perhaps a few women joined the men in this.

25. Vine Deloria Jr., "Traditional Technology," *Winds of Change* 5 (2, Spring 1990): 16.

26. Ibid.

27. Vine Deloria Jr., "Knowing and Understanding: Transitional Education in the Modern World," *Winds of Change* 5 (3, Summer 1990): 16.

28. Ibid., 18.

29. Ibid.

30. Ibid.

31. Vine Deloria Jr., "Out of Chaos," *Parabola* 10 (2, May 1985), 22.

32. Vine Deloria Jr., "Higher Education and Self-Determination," *Winds of Change* 6 (1, Winter 1991): 21.

33. Elizabeth Cook-Lynn, "You May Consider Speaking about Your Art . . . ," in *I Tell You Now: Autobiographical Essays by Native American Writers* (Lincoln: University of Nebraska Press, 1987), 58.

34. Ibid.

35. Simon J. Ortiz, *From Sand Creek* (New York: Thunder's Mouth, 1981), 2.

36. McKale, "Interview," 54.

37. Vine Deloria Jr., interview by the author, Tucson, August 5, 1989.

38. Vine Deloria Jr., foreword to *New and Old Voices of Wah'Kon-Tah*, ed. Robert K. Dodge and Joseph B. McCullough (New York: International, 1985), ix.

39. Ibid., x.

40. Beth Brant, ed., *A Gathering of Spirit: A Collection by North American Indian Women* (Rockland, Maine: Sinister Wisdom, 1984).

41. Brant, *Gathering*, 235, 238.

42. Deloria, foreword to *New and Old Voices*, x.

43. Jimmie Durham, "Those Dead Guys for a Hundred Years," in *I Tell You Now*, 162.

44. Ibid., 163.

45. Ibid., 163-64.

46. Wendy Rose, "Neon Scars," in *I Tell You Now*, ed. Swann and Krupat, 249-69; Paula Gunn Allen, *The Sacred Hoop: Recovering the Feminine in American Indian Traditions* (Boston: Beacon, 1986), 175ff.

47. Bruchac, interview with Wendy Rose, in *Survival This Way*, 252.

48. Ibid., 254, 258.

49. Rose, "Neon Scars," 253.

50. Ibid., 253, 259.

51. Ibid., 260.

52. Ibid., 261.

53. Bruchac, interview with Wendy Rose, in *Survival This Way*, 256-57.

54. Wendy Rose, "Builder Kachina," in *Lost Copper*, by Rose (Banning, Calif.: Malki Museum, 1980), 127.

55. Ibid.

56. Two of the recent books on this are Will Roscoe, coordinating ed., *Living the Spirit: A Gay American Indian Anthology* (New York: St. Martin's, 1988); and Walter Williams, *The Spirit and the Flesh: Sexual Diversity in American Indian Culture* (Boston: Beacon, 1986). Gay and lesbian American Indian people are more and more coming into the purview of American Indian politics, especially in urban areas. Though reception has not been as positive as it should be, Indian people seem to be willing at least to tolerate gay American Indian groups.

57. M. Annette Jaimes with Theresa Halsey, "American Indian Women at the Center of Indigenous Resistance in Contemporary Native America," in *The State of Native America: Genocide, Colonization, and Resistance*, ed. M. Annette Jaimes (Boston: South End, 1991), 334-36.

58. Alex Haley, epilogue to *The Autobiography of Malcolm X* (New York: Grove, 1965), 424; Alice Walker, "In Search of Our Mothers' Gardens," in *In Search of Our Mothers' Gardens: Womanist Prose* (New York: Harcourt Brace Jovanovich, 1983), 231-43.

59. Joy Harjo, "Anchorage," in *She Had Some Horses*, by Harjo (New York: Thunder's Mouth, 1983), 15.

60. Vine Deloria Jr., "It is a Good Day to Die," *Katallagete* 4 (2-3, Fall-Winter 1972): 65.

Bibliography

Alexie, Sherman. *The Business of Fancydancing.* Brooklyn: Hanging Loose, 1992.

Allen, Paula Gunn. *The Sacred Hoop: Recovering the Feminine in American Indian Traditions.* Boston: Beacon, 1986.

_____. *Shadow Country.* Foreword Kenneth Lincoln. Native American Series. Los Angeles: University of California Press, 1982.

_____. *Skins and Bones: Poems 1979-1987.* Los Angeles: West End, 1988.

_____, ed. *Spider Woman's Granddaughters: Traditional Tales and Contemporary Writing by Native American Women.* Boston: Beacon, 1989.

_____. *The Woman Who Owned the Shadows.* San Francisco: Spinsters/Aunt Lute, 1983.

Apess, William. *On Our Own Ground: The Complete Writings of William Apess, a Pequot.* Ed. Barry O'Connell. Amherst: University of Massachusetts Press, 1992.

Bailey, Garrick. "John Joseph Mathews." In *American Indian Intellectuals: 1976 Proceedings of the American Ethnological Society,* ed. Margot Liberty. St. Paul: West, 1978. 205-16.

Baldridge, William. "Toward a Native American Theology." *American Baptist Quarterly* 8 (December 1989): 227-38.

Barnes, Jim. *The American Book of the Dead.* Urbana: University of Illinois Press, 1982.

_____. *La Plata Cantata: Poems.* West Lafayette, Ind.: Purdue University Press, 1989.

Biolsi, Thomas. *Organizing the Lakota: The Political Economy of the New Deal on the Pine Ridge and Rosebud Reservations.* Tucson: University of Arizona Press, 1992.

Blaeser, Kimberly M. "Gerald Vizenor: Writing—In the Oral Tradition." Ph.D. dissertation, University of Notre Dame, 1990.

_____. "Learning 'The Language the Presidents Speak': Images and Issues of Literacy in American Indian Literature." *World Literature Today* 66 (2, Spring 1992): 230-35.

"Books by Iroquois Authors (Mohawk, Seneca, Cayuga, Tuscarora, Oneida, and Onondaga)." *American Indian Quarterly* 6 (3-4, Fall-Winter 1982): 358-76.

Brant, Beth. *Mohawk Trail.* New York: Firebrand, 1985.

_____, ed. *A Gathering of Spirit: A Collection by North American Indian Women.* Rockland, Maine: Sinister Wisdom, 1984.

Brown, Dee. *Bury My Heart at Wounded Knee: An Indian History of the American West.* New York: Holt, Rinehart, Winston, 1970.

Bruchac, Joseph III, ed. *American Indian Writings.* Special issue of *The Greenfield Review* 9 (3-4, 1981-82).

_____, ed. *Songs from This Earth on Turtle's Back: Contemporary American Indian Poetry.* Greenfield Center, N.Y.: Greenfield Review, 1983.

_____, ed. *Survival This Way: Interviews with Native American Writers.* Tucson: University of Arizona Press, 1988.

Burns, Diane. *Riding the One-Eyed Ford.* Bowling Green, N.Y.: Contact II, 1981.

Cameron, Barbara. "Gee, You Don't Seem like an Indian from the Reservation." In *This Bridge Called My Back: Writings by Radical Women of Color,* ed. Cherríe Moraga and Gloria Anzaldúa. 2d ed. New York: Kitchen Table/Women of Color, 1983. 46-52.

Carr, A. A. *Eye Killers.* Norman: University of Oklahoma Press, in press.

Carter, Joseph H. *Never Met a Man I Didn't Like: The Life and Writings of Will Rogers.* New York: Avon, 1991.

Chief Eagle, Dallas. *Winter Count.* Colorado Springs, Colo.: Denton-Berkeland, 1967.

Chrystos. "I Don't Understand Those Who Have Turned Away from Me." In *This Bridge Called My Back: Writings by Radical Women of Color,* ed. Cherríe Moraga and Gloria Anzaldúa. 2d ed. New York: Kitchen Table/Women of Color, 1983. 68-70.

_____. *In Her I Am.* Vancouver, B.C.: Press Gang, 1993.

_____. "No Rock Scorns Me as Whore." In *This Bridge Called My Back: Writings by Radical Women of Color,* ed. Cherríe Moraga and Gloria Anzaldúa. 2d ed. New York: Kitchen Table/Women of Color, 1983. 243-45.

_____. *Not Vanishing.* Vancouver, B.C.: Press Gang, 1988.

Churchill, Ward. *Fantasies of the Master Race: Literature, Cinema, and the Colonization of American Indians,* ed. M. Annette Jaimes. Monroe, Maine: Common Courage, 1992.

_____. "I Am Indigenist." In *Struggle for the Land: A Land Rights Reader.* Monroe, Maine: Common Courage, 1993. 403-51.

_____. *Indians Are Us? Culture and Genocide in Native North America.* Monroe, Maine: Common Courage, 1994.

_____, ed. *Marxism and Native Americans.* Boston: South End, 1984.

_____. "The New Racism: A Critique of James A. Clifton's *The Invented Indian.*" *Wicazo Sa Review* 7 (1, Spring 1991): 51-59.

_____. "White Studies: The Intellectual Imperialism of Contemporary U.S. Education." *Integrateducation* 19 (1-2, 1982): 51-57.

Churchill, Ward, and Sam Gill. "Commentary and Debate." *American Indian Culture and Research Journal* 12 (3, 1988): 49-67.

Churchill, Ward, and Jim Vander Wall. *Agents of Repression: The FBI's Secret War against the Black Panther Party and the American Indian Movement.* Boston: South End, 1988.

Cone, James H. *Malcolm and Martin and America: A Dream or a Nightmare.* Maryknoll, N.Y.: Orbis, 1991.

Cook-Lynn, Elizabeth. *From the River's Edge.* Boston: Little, Brown, 1991.

_____. "The Radical Conscience in American Indian Studies." *Wicazo Sa Review* 7 (1, Fall 1991): 1-8.

_____. "The Rise of the Academic 'Chiefs.' " *Wicazo Sa Review* 2 (1, Spring 1986): 38-40.

_____, ed. Special Issue on Peyotism. *Wicazo Sa Review* 7 (1, Spring 1991).

_____. *Then Badger Said This.* New York: Vantage, 1977. 2d ed. Fairfield, Wash.: Ye Galleon, 1983.

_____. "You May Consider Speaking about Your Art . . . " In *I Tell You Now: Autobiographical Essays by Native American Writers,* ed. Brian Swann and Arnold Krupat. Lincoln: University of Nebraska Press, 1987. 55-64.

Copway, George. *The Traditional History and Characteristic Sketches of the Ojibway Nation.* London: Gelpin, 1850. Repub. as *Indian Life and Indian History, by an Indian Author: Embracing the Traditions of the North American Indian Tribes Regarding Themselves, Particularly the Most Important of All the Tribes, the Ojibways.* 1858. New York: AMS, 1977.

Council on Interracial Books for Children, ed. *Chronicles of American Indian Protest.* Greenwich, Conn.: Fawcett, 1971.

Crosby, Alfred W., Jr. *The Columbian Exchange: Biological and Cultural Consequences of 1492.* Westport, Conn.: Greenwood, 1972.

_____. *Ecological Imperialism: The Biological Expansion of Europe, 900-1900.* Cambridge: Cambridge University Press, 1986.

Cruse, Harold. *The Crisis of the Negro Intellectual: From Its Origins to the Present.* New York: Morrow, 1967.

Deloria, Ella Cara. *Dakota Texts.* 1932. Reprint, Vermillion: University of South Dakota Press, 1992.

_____. *Speaking of Indians.* New York: Friendship, 1944; Vermillion: University of South Dakota Press, 1992.

_____. *Waterlily.* Lincoln: University of Nebraska Press, 1988.

Deloria, Vine, Jr. "American Indians and the Moral Community." *Church and Society* 3 (September-October 1988): 27-38.

_____. *Behind the Trail of Broken Treaties: An Indian Declaration of Independence.* New York: Delacorte, 1974.

_____. "Civilization and Isolation." *North American Review* 263 (2, Summer 1978): 11-14.

_____. "Completing the Theological Circle: Civil Religion in America." *Religious Education* 71 (3, 1976): 278-87.

_____. "The Country Was a Lot Better Off When the Indians Were Running It." *New York Times Magazine,* March 8, 1970. Reprinted in *Red Power,* ed. Alvin

Josephy. New York: McGraw-Hill, 1971; Lincoln: University of Nebraska Press, 1985. 235-47.

_____. *Custer Died for Your Sins: An American Indian Manifesto.* New York: Macmillan, 1969.

_____. *Custer Died for Your Sins: An Indian Manifesto.* New preface. Norman: University of Oklahoma Press, 1988. vii-xiii.

_____. "Custer Died for Your Sins." *Playboy* 16 (8, August, 1969): 131-32+.

_____. "Escaping from Bankruptcy: The Future of the Theological Task." *Katallagete* 6 (1, Summer 1976): 5-9.

_____. Foreword to *New and Old Voices of Wah'Kon-Tah*, ed. Robert K. Dodge and Joseph B. McCullough. New York: International, 1985. ix-x.

_____. *God Is Red.* New York: Grosset and Dunlap, 1973.

_____. *God Is Red: A Native View of Religion.* 2d ed. Golden, Colo.: North American, 1992.

_____. "Higher Education and Self-Determination." *Winds of Change* 6 (1, Winter 1991): 18-25.

_____. *The Indian Affair.* New York: Friendship, 1974.

_____. "Indian Affairs 1973: Hebrews 13:8." *North American Review* (Winter 1973): 108-12.

_____. "The Indian Movement: Out of a Wounded Past." *Ramparts* 13 (March 1975): 28-32.

_____. "Indian Studies—The Orphan of Academia." *Wicazo Sa Review* 2 (2, Fall 1986): 1-9.

_____. *Indians of the Pacific Northwest: From the Coming of the White Man to the Present Day.* Garden City, N.Y.: Doubleday, 1977.

_____. Introduction to *The Red Man in the New World Drama: A Politico-Legal Study with a Pageantry of American Indian History*, by Jennings C. Wise. Rev. and ed. Vine Deloria Jr. Washington, D.C.: W. F. Roberts, 1931; New York: Macmillan, 1971.

_____. "It Is a Good Day to Die." *Katallagete* 4 (2-3, Fall-Winter 1972): 62-65.

_____. "Knowing and Understanding: Transitional Education in the Modern World." *Winds of Change* 5 (3, Summer 1990): 10-15.

_____. "Landlord to Welfare Client: The Decline of the Indian in National Consciousness." *Humboldt Journal of Social Relations* 10 (1, Fall-Winter 1982-83): 116-28.

_____. Letter to the author, April 5, 1991.

_____. Letter to the author, June 22, 1991.

_____. *Metaphysics of Modern Existence.* San Francisco: Harper and Row, 1979.

_____. "A Native American Perspective on Liberation." *Occasional Bulletin of Missionary Research* 1 (3, July 1977): 15-17.

_____. "Native Americans: The American Indian Today." *Annals of the American Academy of Political and Social Sciences* 454 (March 1981): 139-49.

_____. "Non-Violence in American Society." *Katallagete* 5 (2, Winter 1974): 4-7.

_____. "Out of Chaos." *Parabola* 10 (2, May 1985): 14-22.

_____. "Perceptions and Maturity: Reflections on Paul Feyerabend's Point of View." In *Beyond Reason: Essays on the Philosophy of Paul Feyerabend*, ed. Gonzalo Munevar, Dordrecht; Boston: Kluwer Academic, 1991. 389-401.

_____. "The Perpetual Education Report." *Winds of Change* 6 (2, Spring 1991): 12-18.

_____. "Property and Self-Government as Educational Initiatives." *Winds of Change* 5 (4, Autumn 1990): 26-31.

_____. "Religion and Revolution among American Indians." *Worldview* 17 (1, January 1974): 12-15.

_____. "The Theological Dimension of the Indian Protest Movement." *Christian Century* 90 (September 19, 1973): 912-14.

_____. "Traditional Education in the Modern World." *Winds of Change* 5 (1, Winter 1990): 12-18.

_____. "Traditional Technology." *Winds of Change* 5 (2, Spring 1990): 12-17.

_____. "Vision and Community: A Native American Voice." In *Yearning to Breathe Free: Liberation Theologies in the United States*, ed. Mar Peter-Raoul, Linda Rennie Forcey, and Robert Frederick Hunter Jr. Maryknoll, N.Y.: Orbis, 1990. 71-79.

_____. *We Talk, You Listen: New Tribes, New Turf.* New York: Macmillan, 1970.

_____. "Why the U.S. Never Fought the Indians." *Christian Century* 93 (January 7-14, 1976): 9-12.

_____. "Worshiping the Golden Calf: Freedom of Religion in Scalia's America." *New World Outlook* 52 (1, September-October 1991): 22-24.

_____, ed. *American Indian Policy in the Twentieth Century*. Norman: University of Oklahoma Press, 1985.

_____, ed. *Of Utmost Good Faith*. San Francisco: Straight Arrow, 1971.

_____, ed. *A Sender of Words: Essays in Honor of John G. Neihardt*. Salt Lake City: Howe Brothers, 1984.

Deloria, Vine, Jr., and Clifford Lytle. *The Nations Within: The Past and Future of American Indian Sovereignty*. New York: Pantheon, 1984.

"Discussion." *American Indian Culture and Research Journal* 2 (1-2 1978): 28-46.

Dorris, Michael. *The Broken Cord: A Family's Ongoing Struggle with Fetal Alcohol Syndrome*. New York: Harper and Row, 1989.

_____. *A Yellow Raft in Blue Water*. New York: Henry Holt, 1987.

Drinnon, Richard. *Facing West: The Metaphysics of Indian-Hating and Empire Building*. Minneapolis: University of Minnesota Press, 1980.

Durham, Jimmie. "American Indian Culture: Traditionalism and Spiritualism in a Revolutionary Struggle." Unpublished essay, n.d.

_____. "Those Dead Guys for a Hundred Years." In *I Tell You Now: Autobiographical Essays by Native American Writers*, ed. Brian Swann and Arnold Krupat. Lincoln: University of Nebraska Press, 1987. 155-65.

Eastman, Charles A. *From the Deep Woods to Civilization: Chapters in the Autobiography of an Indian*. Boston: Little, Brown, 1916, 1936; Lincoln: University of Nebraska Press, 1977.

——. *Indian Boyhood.* New York: McClure Phillips, 1902.

——. *Old Indian Days.* 1907. Introd. A. LaVonne Brown Ruoff. Lincoln: University of Nebraska Press, 1991.

——. *The Soul of the Indian: An Interpretation.* Boston: Little, Brown, 1911.

Eastman, Charles, and Elaine Goodale Eastman. *Wigwam Evenings: Sioux Folk Tales Retold.* Boston: Little, Brown, 1909; Lincoln: University of Nebraska Press, 1990.

Edmunds, R. David. *The Shawnee Prophet.* Lincoln: University of Nebraska Press, 1982.

Erdrich, Louise. *Baptism of Desire.* New York: Harper and Row, 1989.

——. *The Beet Queen.* New York: Henry Holt, 1986.

——. *The Bingo Palace.* New York: HarperCollins, 1994.

——. *Jacklight.* New York: Holt, Rinehart, Winston, 1984.

——. *Love Medicine.* New York: Holt, Rinehart, Winston, 1984.

——. *Love Medicine.* New and expanded edition. New York. HarperCollins, 1993.

——. *Tracks.* New York: Henry Holt, 1988.

——. "A Writer's Sense of Place." In *A Place of Sense: Essays in Search of the Midwest,* ed. Michael Martone. Iowa City: University of Iowa Press, 1988. 35-44.

Erdrich, Louise, and Michael Dorris. *The Crown of Columbus.* New York: HarperCollins, 1991.

Ewers, John C. "Richard Sanderville, Blackfoot Indian Interpreter." In *American Indian Intellectuals: 1976 Proceedings of the American Ethnological Society,* ed. Margot Liberty. St. Paul: West, 1978. 117-28.

Fanon, Frantz. *Studies in a Dying Colonialism.* Trans. Haakon Chevalier. New York: Grove, 1965.

——. *The Wretched of the Earth.* Trans. Constance Farrington. New York: Grove, 1963.

Feyerabend, Paul. *Against Method.* 1975. Rev. ed., London: Verso, 1988.

Fiedler, Leslie. *The Return of the Vanishing American.* New York: Stein and Day, 1969.

Fisher, Alice Poindexter. "The Transformation of Tradition: A Study of Zitkala-Sa (Bonnin) and Mourning Dove, Two Traditional Indian Writers." Ph.D. Dissertation, City University of New York, 1979.

Fisher, Dexter. Introduction to *Cogewea: The Half-Blood,* by Mourning Dove. Lincoln: University of Nebraska Press, 1981. v-xxix.

Fixico, Donald. *Termination and Relocation: Federal Indian Policy, 1945-1960.* Albuquerque: University of New Mexico Press, 1986.

Forbes, Jack. "Colonialism and Native American Literature: Analysis." *Wicazo Sa Review* 3 (1987): 17-23.

——. *Native Americans and Nixon: Presidential Politics and Minority Self-Determination, 1969-1972.* Los Angeles: University of California-American Indian Studies Center, 1981.

_____, ed. *The Indian in America's Past*. Englewood Cliffs, N.J.: Prentice-Hall, 1964.

Fortunate Eagle, Adam. *Alcatraz, Alcatraz: The Indian Occupation of 1969-1971*. Berkeley: Heyday, 1992.

France, Anatole. "Our Lady's Juggler." In *Golden Tales of Anatole France*. New York: Dodd, Mead, 1927. 102-13.

Francisco, Nia. *Blue Horses for Navajo Women*. Greenfield Center: Greenfield Review, 1988.

Gates, Henry Louis, Jr. *Figures in Black: Words, Signs, and the Racial Self*. New York: Oxford University Press, 1987.

_____. *The Signifying Monkey: An Afro-American Theory of Literary Criticism*. New York: Oxford University Press, 1988.

_____, ed. *"Race" Writing and Difference*. Chicago: University of Chicago Press, 1986. This volume reprints the entire contents of *Critical Inquiry* 12 (Autumn 1985) and 13 (Autumn 1986).

Gridley, Marion. *Contemporary American Indian Leaders*. New York: Dodd, Mead, 1972.

Haley, Alex. *The Autobiography of Malcolm X*. New York: Grove, 1965.

Harjo, Joy. *In Mad Love and War*. Middletown, Conn.: Wesleyan University Press, 1990.

_____. *She Had Some Horses*. New York: Thunder's Mouth, 1983.

Hertzberg, Hazel. *The Search for an American Indian Identity: Modern Pan-Indian Movements*. Syracuse, N.Y.: Syracuse University Press, 1971.

Hobson, Geary, ed. *The Remembered Earth: An Anthology of Contemporary Native American Literature*. Albuquerque: Red Earth, 1979.

Hunter, Carol. "The Historical Context in John Joseph Mathews' *Sundown*," *MELUS* 9 (Spring 1982): 61-72.

_____. "The Protagonist as a Mixed-Blood in John Joseph Mathews's Novel: *Sundown*." *American Indian Quarterly* 6 (3-4, Fall-Winter 1982): 319-36.

Iktomi (Ivan Drift). *America Needs Indians*. Denver: Bradford-Robinson, 1937.

Iverson, Peter. *Carlos Montezuma and the Changing World of American Indians*. Albuquerque: University of New Mexico Press, 1982.

Jaimes, M. Annette. "American Indian Studies: Toward an Indigenous Model." *American Indian Culture and Research Journal* 11 (3, 1987): 1-16.

Jaimes, M. Annette, with Theresa Halsey. "American Indian Women at the Center of Indigenous Resistance in Contemporary Native America." In *The State of Native America: Genocide, Colonization, and Resistance*, ed. M. Annette Jaimes, Boston: South End, 1991. 311-44.

Josephy, Alvin, ed. *Red Power*. New York: McGraw-Hill, 1971; Lincoln: University of Nebraska Press, 1985.

Kenny, Maurice. *Between Two Rivers: Selected Poems 1956-1984*. Fredonia, N.Y.: White Pine, 1987.

_____. *Greyhounding This America*. Chico, Calif.: Heidelberg Graphics, 1988.

_____. *Is Summer This Bear?* Saranac Lake, N.Y.: Chauncy, 1985.

King, Thomas. *Green Grass, Running Water.* Boston: Houghton Mifflin, 1993.

Krupat, Arnold. *The Voice in the Margin: Native American Literature and the Canon.* Berkeley: University of California Press, 1989.

Krupat, Arnold, ed. *New Voices in Native American Literary Criticism.* Smithsonian Series of Studies of Native American Literatures. Washington, D.C.: Smithsonian Institution Press, 1993.

LaPointe, Frank. *The Sioux Today.* New York: Crowell-Collier, 1972.

Larson, Charles R. *American Indian Fiction.* Albuquerque: University of New Mexico Press, 1978.

Leopold, Aldo. *A Sand County Almanac.* New York: Oxford University Press, 1949.

Liberty, Margot, ed. *American Indian Intellectuals: 1976 Proceedings of the American Ethnological Society.* St. Paul: West, 1978.

Lincoln, Kenneth. "From Tai-Me to Rainy Mountain: The Makings of American Indian Literature." *American Indian Quarterly* 10 (2, Spring 1986): 101-17.

———. *Native American Renaissance.* Berkeley: University of California Press, 1983.

Littlefield, Daniel F. *Alex Posey: Creek Poet, Journalist, and Humorist.* Lincoln: University of Nebraska Press, 1992.

———. "American Indians, American Scholars, and the American Literary Canon." MAASA presidential address. *American Studies* 33 (Fall 1992): 95-111.

Littlefield, Daniel, Jr., and James Parins, comps. *American Indian and Alaska Native Newspapers and Periodicals, 1826-1924.* Westport, Conn.: Greenwood, 1984.

Lorde, Audre. *Sister Outsider: Essays and Speeches.* Freedom, Calif.: Crossing, 1984.

Mathews, John Joseph. *Life and Death of an Oilman: The Career of E. W. Marland.* Norman: University of Oklahoma Press, 1951.

———. *The Osages: Children of the Middle Waters.* Norman: University of Oklahoma Press, 1961.

———. *Sundown.* New York: Longman, Green, 1934; Norman: University of Oklahoma Press, 1988.

———. *Talking to the Moon: Wildlife Adventures on the Plains and Prairies of Osage Country.* Norman: University of Oklahoma Press, 1945.

———. *Wah'Kon-Tah: The Osage and the White Man's Road.* Norman: University of Oklahoma Press, 1932.

McGraw, James R. "God Is Also Red: An Interview with Vine Deloria, Jr." *Christianity and Crisis* 35 (September 15, 1975): 198-206.

McNickle, D'Arcy. *The Hawk Is Hungry and Other Stories.* Ed. and with intro. by Birgit Hans. Tucson: University of Arizona Press, 1992.

———. *Indian Man: A Life of Oliver La Farge.* Bloomington: Indiana University Press, 1971.

———. *Native American Tribalism: Indian Survival and Renewals.* New York: Oxford University Press, 1973.

———. *The Surrounded.* New York: Dodd, Mead, 1936. Albuquerque: University of New Mexico Press, 1978.

_____. *They Came Here First: The Epic of the American Indian.* Philadelphia: Lippincott, 1949.

_____. *Wind from an Enemy Sky.* 1978. Albuquerque: University of New Mexico Press, 1988.

Miller, David Humphreys. *Ghost Dance.* 1959. Reprint, Lincoln: University of Nebraska Press, 1985.

Miller, David R. "Charles Alexander Eastman, the 'Winner': From Deep Woods to Civilization." In *American Indian Intellectuals: 1976 Proceedings of the American Ethnological Society,* ed. Margot Liberty. St. Paul: West, 1978. 61-74.

Milsten, David Randolph. *The Cherokee Kid.* West Chicago, Ill.: Glenheath, 1987.

Momaday, N. Scott. *The Ancient Child.* New York: Doubleday, 1989.

_____. *House Made of Dawn.* New York: Harper and Row, 1968.

_____. "The Man Made of Words." Reprinted in *The Remembered Earth: An Anthology of Contemporary Native American Literature,* ed. Geary Hobson. Albuquerque: Red Earth, 1979. 162-173.

_____. *The Names.* New York: Harper and Row, 1976.

_____. *The Way to Rainy Mountain.* Albuquerque: University of New Mexico Press, 1969.

Montezuma, Carlos. "The Repression of the Indian." *Wassaja* 5 (March 12, 1921), 2.

Moraga, Cherríe, and Gloria Anzaldúa, eds. *This Bridge Called My Back: Writings by Radical Women of Color.* 2d ed. New York: Kitchen Table/Women of Color, 1983.

Mourning Dove. *Cogewea: The Half-Blood.* 1927. Reprint, Lincoln: University of Nebraska Press, 1981.

_____. *Coyote Stories,* ed. Heister Dean Guie. Caldwell, Idaho: Caxton, 1933; Lincoln: University of Nebraska Press, 1990, ed. Jay Miller.

Murphy, James E., and Sharon M. Murphy. *Let My People Know: American Indian Journalism.* Norman: University of Oklahoma Press, 1981.

Neihardt, John G. *Black Elk Speaks: Being the Life of a Holy Man of the Oglala Sioux.* 1932. Reprint, Lincoln: University of Nebraska Press, 1961.

Niatum, Duane, ed. *Harper's Anthology of 20th Century Native American Poetry.* New York: Harper and Row, 1988.

Ortiz, Roxanne Dunbar. "Developing Academic Indian Professionals: A Proposal." *Wicazo Sa Review* 1 (1, Spring 1985): 5-9.

_____. Foreword to *Native Americans and Nixon: Presidential Politics and Minority Self-Determination, 1969-1972,* by Jack Forbes. Los Angeles: University of California-American Indian Studies Center, 1981. 1-23.

_____. "The Fourth World and Indigenism: Politics of Isolation and Alternatives." *Journal of Ethnic Studies* 12 (1, Spring 1984): 79-105.

_____. *The Great Sioux Nation: Sitting in Judgment on America.* New York: American Indian Treaty Council Information Center, 1977.

Ortiz, Simon J. *From Sand Creek.* New York: Thunder's Mouth, 1981.

_____. *Woven Stone.* Tucson: University of Arizona Press, 1992.

_____, ed. *Earth Power Coming: Short Fiction in Native American Literature*. Tsaile, Ariz.: Navajo Community College Press, 1983.

Owens, Louis. *Other Destinies: Understanding the American Indian Novel*. Norman: University of Oklahoma Press, 1992.

_____. *The Sharpest Sight*. American Indian Literature and Critical Studies Series 1. Norman: University of Oklahoma Press, 1991.

_____. *Wolfsong*. Albuquerque, N. Mex.: West End, 1991.

Parins, James W. *John Rollin Ridge: His Life and Works*. Lincoln: University of Nebraska Press, 1991.

Parker, Dorothy S. "D'Arcy McNickle: An Annotated Bibliography of His Published Articles and Book Reviews in a Biographical Context." *American Indian Culture and Research Journal* 14 (2, 1990): 55-75.

_____. *Singing an Indian Song: A Biography of D'Arcy McNickle*. Lincoln: University of Nebraska Press, 1992.

Peter-Raoul, Mar, Linda Rennie Forcey, and Robert Frederick Hunter Jr., eds. *Yearning to Breathe Free: Liberation Theologies in the United States*. Maryknoll, N.Y.: Orbis, 1990.

Peyer, Bernd, ed. *The Elders Wrote: An Anthology of Early Prose by North American Indians, 1768-1931*. Berlin: Dietrich Reimer Verlag, 1982.

_____, ed. *The Singing Spirit: Early Short Stories by North American Indians*. Tucson: University of Arizona Press, 1989.

Pieris, Aloysius. *An Asian Theology of Liberation*. Maryknoll, N.Y.: Orbis, 1988.

Posey, Alexander. *The Fus Fixico Letters*, ed. Daniel F. Littlefield Jr. and Carol A. Petty Hunter. Lincoln: University of Nebraska Press, 1993.

_____. *The Poems of Alexander Lawrence Posey*. Ed. Mrs. Minnie H. Posey. Memoir by William Elsey Connelly. Topeka: Crane, 1910.

Prucha, Francis Paul. *The Great Father: The United States Government and the American Indians*. Lincoln: University of Nebraska Press, 1984; abr. ed., Lincoln: University of Nebraska Press, 1986.

Reuther, Rosemary Radford. *Sexism and God-Talk: Toward a Feminist Theology*. Boston: Beacon, 1983.

Revard, Carter. *An Eagle Nation*. Tucson: University of Arizona Press, 1993.

_____. *Ponca War Dancers*. Norman, Okla.: Point Riders, 1980.

Roscoe, Will, coordinating ed. *Living the Spirit: A Gay American Indian Anthology*. New York: St. Martin's, 1988.

Rose, Wendy. *Bone Dance: New and Selected Poems, 1965-1993*. Tucson: University of Arizona Press, 1994.

_____. *Going to War with All My Relations: New and Selected Poems*. Flagstaff, Ariz.: Northland, 1993.

_____. *The Halfbreed Chronicles and Other Poems*. Los Angeles: West End, 1985.

_____. *Lost Copper*. Banning, Calif.: Malki Museum, 1980.

_____. "Neon Scars." In *I Tell You Now: Autobiographical Essays by Native American Writers*, ed. Brian Swann and Arnold Krupat. Lincoln: University of Nebraska Press, 1987. 253-61.

Ruoff, A. LaVonne Brown. *American Indian Literatures: An Introduction, Bibliographic Review, and Selected Bibliography.* New York: Modern Language Association, 1990.

_____. "John Joseph Mathews's *Talking to the Moon*: Literary and Osage Contexts." In *Multicultural Autobiography: American Lives,* ed. James Robert Payne. Knoxville: University of Tennessee Press, 1992. 1-31.

_____. "Justice for Indians and Women: The Protest Fiction of Alice Callahan and Pauline Johnson." *World Literature Today* 66 (2, Spring 1992): 249-55.

Said, Edward. *Orientalism.* New York: Pantheon, 1978.

_____. "Orientalism Reconsidered." *Race and Class* 27 (2, Autumn 1985): 1-16.

_____. *The World, the Text, and the Critic.* Cambridge: Harvard University Press, 1983.

_____. "Yeats and Colonialism." In *Nationalism, Colonialism, and Literature,* ed. Terry Eagleton, Fredric Jameson, and Edward Said. Minneapolis: University of Minnesota Press, 1990.

Sarris, Greg. *Keeping Slug Woman Alive: A Holistic Approach to American Indian Texts.* Berkeley: University of California Press, 1993.

Shanley, Katherine S. " 'Only an Indian': The Prose and Poetry of James Welch." Forthcoming.

_____. "Thoughts on Indian Feminism." In *A Gathering of Spirit: A Collection by North American Indian Women,* ed. Beth Brant. Rockland, Maine: Sinister Wisdom, 1984. 213-15.

_____. "Time and Time-Again: Notes Toward an Understanding of Radical Elements in American Indian Fiction." In *Transforming the Curriculum: Ethnic Studies and Women's Studies.* Ed. Johnnella E. Butler and John C. Walter. Albany: State University of New York Press, 1991. 243-56.

Shorris, Earl. *The Death of the Great Spirit: An Elegy for the American Indian.* New York: Simon and Schuster, 1971.

Silko, Leslie Marmon. *Almanac of the Dead.* New York: Simon and Schuster, 1991.

_____. *Ceremony.* New York: Viking Press, 1977.

_____. *Storyteller.* New York: Seaver Books, 1981.

Smith, Paul Chaat. "American Indian Movement." *Encyclopedia of the American Left.* New York: Garland, 1990. 22-23.

Smith, Paul Chaat, and Robert Allen Warrior. *Like a Hurricane: How Wounded Knee II Changed Indian America.* New York: New Press, in press.

Smith, Richard Chase, and Shelton H. Davis. "Commentary on Roxanne Dunbar Ortiz's 'The Fourth World and Indigenism: Politics of Isolation and Alternatives.' " *Journal of Ethnic Studies* 12 (3, Winter 1985): 113-20.

Smith, Steven Ray. "Limousine to Las Montanas." *Aura Literary/Arts Review* 27 (Fall-Winter 1989): 42-55.

Spivak, Gayatri Chakravorty. *In Other Worlds: Essays in Cultural Politics.* New York: Routledge, 1988.

Steiner, Stan. *The New Indians.* New York: Harper and Row, 1968.

Swann, Brian, and Arnold Krupat, eds. *I Tell You Now: Autobiographical Essays by Native American Writers*. Lincoln: University of Nebraska Press, 1987.

Tapahanso, Luci. *A Breeze Swept Through*. Los Angeles: West End, 1987.

_____. *Saani Dahataal: The Women are Singing*. Tucson: University of Arizona Press, 1993.

Thompson, Hunter S. "Marlon Brando and the Indian Fish-In." In Thompson, *The Great Shark Hunt: Gonzo Papers*. Vol. 1. New York: Summit, 1979. 440-46.

Tinker, George. "God, Gods, Goddesses, and Mystery." Unpublished essay, 1990.

_____. "The Integrity of Creation: Restoring Trinitarian Balance." *The Ecumenical Review* 41 (4, 1989): 527-36.

Tsosie, Rebecca. "Surviving the War by Singing the Blues: The Contemporary Ethos of American Indian Political Poetry." *American Indian Culture and Research Journal* 10 (3, 1986): 25-51.

Vizenor, Gerald. *Crossbloods: Bone Courts, Bingo, and Other Reports*. Minneapolis: University of Minnesota Press, 1990.

_____. *Darkness in Saint Louis Bearheart*. 1977. Reprinted as *Bearheart: The Heirship Chronicles*. Minneapolis: University of Minnesota Press, 1990.

_____. *Earthdivers: Tribal Narratives on Mixed Descent*. Minneapolis: University of Minnesota Press, 1981.

_____. *Empty Swings: Haiku in English*. With Japanese calligraphy by Haruko Isobe. Minneapolis: Nodin, 1967.

_____. *Griever: An American Monkey King in China*. Minneapolis: University of Minnesota Press, 1987.

_____. *The Heirs of Columbus*. Hanover, N.H.: University Press of New England, 1991.

_____. *Interior Landscapes: Autobiographical Myths and Metaphors*. Minneapolis: University of Minnesota Press, 1990.

_____. *Manifest Manners: Postindian Warriors of Survivance*. Hanover, N.H.: University Press of New England, 1994.

_____. *Seventeen Chirps: Haiku in English*. Minneapolis: Nodin, 1964.

_____. *The Trickster of Liberty*. Minneapolis: University of Minnesota Press, 1988.

_____. *Wordarrows: Indians and Whites in the New Fur Trade*. Minneapolis: University of Minnesota Press, 1978.

_____, ed. *The Everlasting Sky: New Voices from the People Named the Chippewa*. New York: Macmillan, 1972.

_____, ed. *Narrative Chance: Postmodern Discourse on Native American Indian Literatures*. Albuquerque: University of New Mexico Press, 1989.

_____, ed. *Summer in the Spring: Lyric Poems of the Ojibway*. Minneapolis: Nodin, 1965.

_____, ed. *Summer in the Spring: Anishinaabe Lyric Poems and Stories*. Revised edition. Norman: University of Oklahoma Press, 1993.

Walker, Alice. "In Search of Our Mothers' Gardens." In *In Search of Our Mothers' Gardens: Womanist Prose*. New York: Harcourt Brace Jovanovich, 1983. 231-43.

Warrior, Clyde. "We Are Not Free." In *Red Power*, ed. Alvin Josephy. New York: McGraw-Hill, 1971; Lincoln: University of Nebraska Press, 1985. 71-77.

Warrior, Robert Allen. "Canaanites, Cowboys, and Indians: Deliverance, Conquest, and Liberation Theology Today." *C & C* 49 (September 12, 1989): 261-65.

_____. "Dances with Ghosts: Pain and Suffering on the Big Foot Trail." *Village Voice* (January 15, 1991): 33-37.

_____. "Dancing with Wastes." *C & C* 51 (July 15, 1991): 216-17.

_____. "Indian Issues and Romantic Solidarity." *C & C* 51 (February 4, 1991): 8-10.

_____. "Reflections from the War Zone." In *Collateral Damage: The New World Order at Home and Abroad*, ed. Cynthia Peters. Boston: South End, 1992. 299-304.

Welch, Deborah Sue. "Zitkala-Sa: An American Indian Leader, 1876-1938." Unpublished dissertation. University of Wyoming, 1985.

Welch, James. *The Death of Jim Loney*. New York: Harper and Row, 1979.

_____. *The Indian Lawyer*. New York: Norton, 1990.

_____. *Winter in the Blood*. New York: Viking, 1974.

West, Cornel. *The American Evasion of Philosophy*. Madison: University of Wisconsin Press, 1989.

_____. *Prophesy Deliverance: An Afro-American Revolutionary Christianity*. Philadelphia: Westminster, 1982.

White, Richard. "American Environmental History: The Development of a New Historical Field." *Pacific Historical Review* 54 (August 1985): 297-335.

Wiget, Andrew. *Native American Literature*. Boston: Twayne, 1985.

Willard, William. "The First Amendment, Anglo-Conformity, and American Indian Religious Freedom." *Wicazo Sa Review* 7 (1, Spring 1991): 26-30.

_____. "A Report on a Colonial Study of an Indigenous Other." Unpublished manuscript, 1991.

_____. "Zitkala-Sa: A Woman Who Would Be Heard." *Wicazo Sa Review* 1 (1, Spring 1985): 11-16.

Willard, William, and Mary Kay Downing. "American Indian Studies and Inter-Cultural Education." *Wicazo Sa Review* 7 (1, Fall 1991): 9-13.

Williams, Walter. *The Spirit and the Flesh: Sexual Diversity in American Indian Culture*. Boston: Beacon, 1986.

Wilson, Edmund. *Apologies to the Iroquois*. New York: Knopf, 1959.

Wilson, Raymond. *Ohiyesa: Charles Eastman, Santee Sioux*. Urbana: University of Illinois Press, 1983.

Wilson, Terry P. "Osage Oxonian: The Heritage of John Joseph Mathews." *Chronicles of Oklahoma* 59 (Fall 1981): 264-93.

_____. *The Underground Reservation: Osage Oil*. Lincoln: University of Nebraska Press, 1985.

_____. "Women of the Osage: A Century of Change, 1874-1982." In *Women in*

Oklahoma: A Century of Change, ed. Melvina K. Thurman. Oklahoma City: Oklahoma State Historical Society, 1982.

Winnemucca, Sarah [Hopkins]. *Life among the Piutes: Their Wrongs and Claims.* Ed. Mrs. Horace Mann. 1883. Bishop: Chalfant, 1969.

Wise, Jennings C. *The Red Man in the New World Drama: A Politico-Legal Study with a Pageantry of American Indian History.* Rev., ed., and with intro. by Vine Deloria Jr. Washington, D.C.: W. F. Roberts, 1931; New York: Macmillan, 1971.

Worster, Donald. *Dust Bowl: The Southern Plains in the 1930s.* Oxford: Oxford University Press, 1979.

_____. *Nature's Economy: A History of Ecological Ideas.* Cambridge: Cambridge University Press, 1977.

Yagoda, Ben. *Will Rogers: A Biography.* New York: Knopf, 1993.

Young Bear, Ray A. *The Invisible Musician: Poems.* Duluth, Minn.: Holy Cow!, 1990.

Zitkala-Sa (Gertrude Bonnin). *American Indian Stories.* 1921. Lincoln: University of Nebraska Press, 1985.

_____. *Old Indian Legends.* 1901. Lincoln: University of Nebraska Press, 1985.

Index

and individualism, 7, 76, 91-92
and intellectual vocation, 126
at Iowa State University, 32
and Judaism, 72, 74-75
at the Kent School, 32
and liberation theology, 140 n. 27
maturity, concept of, 80-82, 88, 104-5
and the National Congress of American
 Indians, 30-31, 93
National Indian Youth Council,
 relationship to, 27, 31, 93
and nationalism, 88-98
at the Pine Ridge Reservation, 31-32
and poetry, American Indian, 116
and pragmatism, 33, 40
and process thought, xxi, 79, 84-85,
 91-98, 105
The Red Man in the New World Drama,
 36, 37
and religious experience, 73-75, 79-80,
 104, 124
and religious phenomena, 73-75, 79
and separatism, 88-98
and sovereignty, 88-98, 103, 111
and traditionalism, 32-34, 84, 88, 94
and treaties, 33, 89
at the University of Colorado, 30, 33
We Talk, You Listen, 36, 90-98
withdrawal, concept of, 92, 111
and Wounded Knee, 1890 massacre of,
 33
and Wounded Knee, 1973 occupation of,
 39-40, 88, 93, 96
diaspora, 35-38, 89, 93
Durham, Jimmie, xvii, 118-19

Eastman, Charles, xix, xx, 4, 5-11, 14, 22,
 24, 132 n. 48
Eastman, Elaine Goodale, 5, 14
ecology, 60, 115
economic class, xiii-xix, 14, 44
essentialism, xvii-xix, 44, 86, 91, 120, 123,
 127 nn. 4, 5
experience, 101, 103, 105, 117, 119

federal policy, 12, 14, 17, 21, 24-25, 41,
 130 n. 25
feminism, xvii, 2, 5, 35, 43-44, 124
Feyerabend, Paul, 80, 115

fishing rights, 26-27, 30, 41, 134 n. 109
freedom of religion, 9-10, 12, 20, 24
friend-of-the-Indian groups, 5, 10, 12, 13
"fumbling toward God." *See* Mathews, John
 Joseph

ga-ni-tha. *See* chaos
gender, xiii, xviii, 9, 44, 63, 103, 108, 114,
 137 n. 164
Ghost Dance, 5, 30, 39, 94
God Is Red. *See* Deloria, Vine, Jr.
Goodale, Elaine. *See* Eastman, Elaine
 Goodale
Great Depression, 21, 22, 23, 52, 59, 100
"Great Frenzy," 17, 49, 59

hard-line political scholarship, xviii, 43
House Made of Dawn (Momaday), 37, 42
Hunter, Carol, 55-56

I Tell You Now (Swann and Krupat, eds.),
 118-20
idealism, xvii, 94
identity, xix, xxi-xxii, 14, 21, 54-56, 77-78,
 82, 120, 127 n. 4
inclusivity, xxii, 44, 86-87, 114, 121-22
Indian Bureau. *See* Bureau of Indian Affairs
Indian New Deal. *See* Indian Reorganization
 Act
Indian Reorganization Act, 14, 20, 23-24,
 32, 59, 132 n. 50
Indian Rights Association, 13, 20
individualism, 7, 76, 91-92
integrationism, xxii, 7, 11, 14, 24, 42
 among African-Americans, 11
intellectual sovereignty, xxiii, 98, 101, 103,
 113-14, 117, 124
interrupted virility, 82, 100
Iowa State University, 32

Jaimes, M. Annette, xvii, xviii, 9, 124
Judaism, 72, 74-75

Kent School, 32

Lake Mohonk Conference, 5, 13
land, xxii, 45, 57, 62, 71, 72, 78, 80, 81-87,
 94, 102, 105-8, 110-11, 122, 123
Larson, Charles, 53, 54, 55

Little Old Men, 108-9, 111-12
Lutheran School of Theology. *See* Augustana
  Theological Seminary

Malcolm X, 11, 36, 125
Mathews, John Joseph:
  Anglophilia of, 23
  biological determinism in the works of,
    98
  biological urge, concept of, 61-62
  biology, laws of, xv, 60-65, 67, 85, 100-
    101, 105
  at the Blackjacks, 23, 58, 60, 65, 68,
    101, 103-4, 106-7, 111-15, 118, 119,
    121, 123
  chaos, concept of, 108-10
  Christianity, Western, critique of, 98
  and Clements, Frederick E., 60, 114
  early milieu, 15
  experience, concept of, 103-4
  fatalism of, 98, 102
  on "fumbling toward God," 109-10
  hunting expedition, North African,
    18-19
  and the Little Old Men, 108-10, 111
  maturity, concept of, 63, 80-82, 84, 86,
    88, 100-101
  and nature writing, xxi, 58
  as "Oklahoma Hemingway," 23
  ornamentation, concept of, 61, 65, 101
  Osage Tribal Council, tenure on, 23-24,
    59
  Osage Tribal Museum, founder of, 24,
    99
  *The Osages; Children of the Middle
    Waters*, 16, 25, 26, 108
  at Oxford University, 18
  peyote/peyotism, relationship to, 24, 58,
    98
  play, concept of, 43, 62, 88, 101
  process, concepts of, 84-85, 99, 102, 113
  progressivism, relation to, 54, 59
  Rhodes Scholarship, 18
  and Sears, Paul, friendship with, 60, 114
  senility, concept of, 63, 82, 83, 84, 100-
    101
  and sexism in the works of, 103
  Sundown, xxii, 23, 45-47, 50-56, 59, 65,
    68, 75, 81-86, 107, 119

  attitude toward, 53
  Talking to the Moon, xiv, 25, 56-68, 70,
    80-85, 101, 111, 114
  at University of Oklahoma, 17
  virility, 62, 63, 67, 81-84, 100, 101
  and visitors to the Blackjacks, xiv-xv
  Wah'Kon-Tah, 22-23, 53
  whiteness, critique of, 67-68
  withdrawal, concept of, 103
  women, portrayal of, 52, 63
  maturity, xiii, 63, 80-82, 84, 86, 88, 100-
    101, 104-5
McNickle, D'Arcy, xv, 21, 22, 25-27, 42,
    55-56, 83
Medicine Root District, 32-33, 135 n. 129
militancy, 30, 35, 37, 39, 90, 92, 94-95, 98
missionaries, 12, 31
Momaday, N. Scott, xvi, xviii, 22, 37, 42,
    60, 137 n. 162
Montezuma, Carlos, 4, 6, 8-10, 12-13, 24
Mourning Dove, 22, 24, 42, 56, 133 n. 88

National Congress of American Indians, 14,
    20-21, 30-31, 33, 28, 40, 42, 93, 133 n.
    77
National Indian Youth Council, 26-31, 35,
    36, 38, 40, 42, 43, 93, 134 n. 109
nationalism, 11, 29, 30, 34, 36-39, 88-90,
    92, 94
  among African-Americans, 11
Native American Church, 10, 12, 131 n. 36
Nixon administration, 38-39
noncooperationism, 4, 12, 54, 81, 83
No'n-Ho'n-Shinka. *See* Little Old Men

Occom, Samson, 3, 44
Ohiyesa. *See* Charles Eastman
Oklahoma, University of, xiv, 17, 18, 48, 60
orgasm. *See* climax
ornamentation, 61, 65, 101
Osage County, 49, 57
Osages:
  Osage National Council, 17, 47, 82, 109
  Osage Reign of Terror, 18
  Osage Tribal Council, 23, 59
  Osage Tribal Museum, 24, 99
  The Osages: Children of the Middle Waters
    (Mathews), 16, 25-26, 108
  Progressives, 46-47, 52-54, 59, 82

Robert Allen Warrior (Osage) teaches American Indian literature and intellectual history in the Department of English at Stanford University. He has covered American Indian political, cultural, and religious issues for the *Village Voice*, the *Progressive*, the *Lakota Times*, *Akwesasne Notes*, *Lies of Our Times*, and numerous other publications. With Paul Chaat Smith, he is completing a book-length journalistic work, *Like a Hurricane: How Wounded Knee II Changed Indian America*.